Colorado
Trout Fishing

Part II
Prime Fishing Locations

Colorado
Trout Fishing

Part II
Prime Fishing Locations

by

Merton D. Leeper

ML Publications
P.O. Box 593
Littleton, CO 80160

Third Printing

     3   4   5   6   7   8   9

Printed in the United States of America.

ISBN 0-9617325-1-2

I wish to dedicate this book to my wife, Mary, who has supported me in my every endeavor. Not only are you my best friend and lover, you are quite a fisherlady! There was never an M&M Connection like us.

Contents

Foreword

Introduction

1—Grand Lake, Shadow Mountain Dam,
and Granby Reservoir 1

2—Eleven Mile Reservoir 15

3—Curecanti National Recreation Area, Blue Mesa,
Morrow Point Dam, and Crystal Reservoir 19

4—Spinney Mountain Reservoir 27

5—Dillon Reservoir 31

6—Green Mountain Dam 45

7—Lake John, North, South,
and East Delaney Buttes 49

8—Steamboat Lake 57

9—Reudi Reservoir 59

10—Twin Lakes Reservoir 63

11—Other Fine Colorado Lakes 69

12—Colorado River Systems 75

13—Introduction to Ice Fishing or
"How I Got Hooked" 79

14—Cleaning, Cooking, and Mounting Trout 87

Foreword

Mert Leeper is well known for his trout fishing expertise throughout Colorado and the United States. This book is his second in a series titled, *Colorado Trout Fishing* and appears to be a winner. Armed with the techniques described in his first book, *Colorado Trout Fishing: Methods and Techniques* and this book detailing exactly where to fish, what to use, and pinpointing these locations on a contour map of each waterway, its hard to go wrong.

Mert has authored two books, written articles on fishing and hunting as a regular columnist for *Western Sportsmen Outdoor News*, been featured on nationally syndicated radio on the In-Fisherman Radio Network, featured as a guest speaker on radio stations KYBG High Country Outdoors and KMDK Outdoors for the Asking. He has been written about by *Fishing and Hunting News* and the *Denver Post*, *Colorado Transcript*, and has had numerous book reviews by the Colorado Division of Wildlife, the Colorado Wildlife Federation, and numerous newspapers throughout Colorado. He was recently given special recognition by the city of Wheat Ridge for his teaching programs given through the Wheat Ridge Recreation Department. Merton can be found at lakeside throughout the state with chalk in hand teaching seminars on trout fishing.

He recently gave a seminar to the 50th Annual Alumni Association at the School of Mines as part of their alumni activities.

His uncanny ability to catch large fish consistently, he says, relates to the unusual attention to every area of fishing—from preparation of equipment, to tying just the right knot (such as the Leeper Keeper Adjusta Hook), and in the application of these techniques at a diverse number of lakes and streams in Colorado make his one of the premier names spoken of when discussing trout fishing in Colorado.

Jim Merriott
"The Jayhawker"
High Country Outdoors

Introduction

Colorado Trout Fishing, Part II tells you *where* 10 percent of the fishermen catch 90 percent of the fish, whereas, *Colorado Trout Fishing: Methods and Techniques* describes *why* 10 percent of the fishermen catch 90 percent of the fish.

Colorado Trout Fishing, Part II, provides detailed information regarding physical or historical data about specific waterways, contour maps, exact fishing locations, bait preference at each location, and what species of trout or salmon to expect to catch at these locations. River systems are described in a narrative format because of the impracticality of contouring thousands of miles of river systems on paper. The exact locations are denoted by intersecting highways and streams. The listed systems are of extreme quality and offer the angler many hours of angling pleasure. Additionally, there are comprehensive chapters on wintertime fishing methods and techniques, a trout recipe and information relating to the cleaning, cooking, and skinning of trout.

The first book *Colorado Trout Fishing: Methods and Techniques*, provides detailed information on the prey, equipment, water phenomena, bait fishing, flyfishing with a spinning rod and a bubble, spin fishing, flyfishing with a flyrod, kokanee salmon and more.

Detailed diagrams throughout the text include: tying a professionally snelled hook: rod and reel repair; how to tie blood knots, blooddroppers, trilene knots, improved clench knots, the Leeper Keeper Adjusta Hook; blowing up worms; easy ways to catch crickets and grasshoppers; volumes of unique fishing techniques for lakes and streams and how to fish for lunker lake trout (Mackinaw).

About the Cover

Vast blue curtains of radiant warmth dot the landscape in the majestic beauty of winter. A time for rejoicing and prayer, Christmas has passed and the new year has come...As I sat on the ice in awe of the mountains overlooking Granby Dam, these thoughts passed through my mind. Just think, millions of years ago, the Colorado mountains housed some of the most fantastic creatures on this Earth, such as the Pterodactyl, Triceratops, "Mr. Rex," and "Tyrannosaurus Macks."

It was so cold this day that my mind wandered off as I began drilling my first of three ice holes. My prey, of course, a "Tyrannosaurus Mack" otherwise known as a Mackinaw (lake trout).

Granby Dam may be the best producer of large macks in the lower forty-eight states. Twenty-pounders are common, while thirty-pounders are uncommonly caught but consistently throughout the year. The record state Mackinaw is surely to come out of this impoundment...a forty-pound mack was gill netted, tagged, and released this year.

Over the past few years, I've become a sort of mack fanatic. While fishing for trout between the outlet of Grand Lake and the inlet to Shadow Mountain Dam, two locals pulled up in a twelve-foot boat and motored toward Grand Lake. Danny, my fishing partner, and I wondered how they were going to fish since the lake was only one-third ice free. Not more than one hour later, these two characters motored back in with four of the largest trout we had ever seen. They were trolling rapalas just under the surface. Danny was sure they would mount these lunkers, but seconds later, they were cleaning the fish.

We knew several trolling methods to use, but didn't have our boat with us. So, after these gents left, we netted the entrails and began dissecting their stomachs. They contained six whole suckers, two small rainbows, and one kokanee salmon. Now, we weren't born on a peanut branch (even though some may think so) because we had ourselves caught and thrown onto the bank several suckers in which we thought had no use at all. We quickly gathered them up and put them in our ice box. Our catch this weekend consisted of nine suckers and sixteen small rainbows.

At home, I can clearly remember my wife, Mary, saying, "Thanks, but no thanks. If you think that I'm going to cook those suckers—you're crazy." The trout were great and the suckers resided in the freezer for further consideration.

One week later, Danny and I took my small twelve-foot boat and began our trip toward Grand Lake. Our arsenal consisted of sucker/carp meat, jointed rapalas, and jigs. The macks wouldn't hit the top water lures, but would readily hit our bait on the bottom rigs and the jigs tipped with sucker or carp filets. This outing netted us four fish of five to nine pounds.

Since this outing (years ago), we have refined and honed our techniques to the point that we can catch Mackinaw year round. Anyway, enough of past history and back to this story.

Danny and I had just finished drilling our six ice holes (two for our graph finders, two for our bottom rigs, and two for our jig rigs) when he spotted a school of fish coming through.

As I lowered my jig through the ice hole, touched the bottom, and slowly jigged, I had an immediate bite. Upon checking my bait, rebaiting, and lowering it down the hole (twice more), I had immediate bites. Frustration was mounting as I pulled my jig up again to rebait—this time I put a large wedge of sucker filet upon the jig. When the jig once again hit the bottom, I felt a pressure and struck hard sinking the single hook deep into the fishes mouth.

I knew that this fish was a good one when the drag payed out at an alarming rate. I wondered if the fish was ever going to stop. The first twenty minutes of this fight, I did not gain an inch of line, soon after, I got a couple of turns on my Mitchell deep spooled 300. An inch turned into feet and finally, I had this Mack near the surface just under the ice. One look at Danny holding the gaff was enough (I think it was Danny, not the gaff that scared this fish). The fish hightailed it into a dogged second run...but this time, for every yard of line taken out, I gained a foot, then two feet. At this point, I looked at Danny, said a prayer, and told him to gaff the fish, ever so carefully. We both knew the fish would exceed twenty pounds and were keenly aware of how many other Mackinaw had gained their freedom at this juncture.

My mind was on one thought only, keep a tight line. Danny lowered the gaff and quickly pulled, I felt the line give way—slack. At this moment, I plunged my hand into the hole, only to hear Danny say, "I've got him!" The slack line was because Danny was pulling this behemoth through the ice hole.

This fish was thirty-six and one-half inches long and had a girth of twenty-eight inches around. The weight was thirty-two pounds and eight ounces, almost a state record.

Arapaho Bay, Granby Dam.

Grand Lake, Shadow Mountain Dam, and Granby Reservoir

Spring in the magnificent Rockies can be compared to volcanic eruptions, the ice age, or a transition of both. From late March to the end of April, it is typical to experience snow, rain, hail, or snow and rain mixed with a lightning storm, and the warm rays of the sun all within a few hours of the day. Meteorological confusion is the rule.

Confusion does not end here though, it spans deep into the populous of the numerous Colorado residents. There are those who have "holed up" all winter seeking the solice of the warmth and solitude of city life and then there are those who have trekked through the bite of winter seeking their prey from ice holes. Both have a paradox.

The wintertime angler must give way to the elements and adjust his mindset toward traditional angling tactics which will take spring trout. Meanwhile, the "holed up for winter angler" comes out of hibernation passionately seeking his prey only to find that the lakes and rivers are still iced up and access is difficult at best. Spring is on the horizon.

The springtime anglers prey primarily centers around those trout which are most active at this time of the year. The combination of water temperatures and the urge to spawn drive the rainbows, cutthroats, and Mackinaw trout into the inlets and bays of all the waterways that house them. In the river systems, the trout move from the deep pools into the riffles which house sandy pebble bottoms that become the playground of several new generations of the anglers forte—trout.

The following charts will focus on the productive areas of Grand Lake, Shadow Mountain Reservoir, and Granby Dam and the connecting river systems that flow into or between these impoundments. Lake fisherman will find only four major open water areas, while the stream fisherman has but three.

Chart I

This chart is to be used in combination with the map of the Granby area.

Locations

	1	2	3	4	5	6	7
A	●	●	●	●	●	●	●
B	●	●	●	●			
C							●
D				●	●	●	●
E	●	●			●	●	
F	●					●	

Type of Trout/Salmon Caught

**TYPE OF TROUT/
SALMON CAUGHT**

A–Rainbow
B–Brown
C–Brook
D–Cutthroat
E–Lake Trout
F–Kokanee Salmon

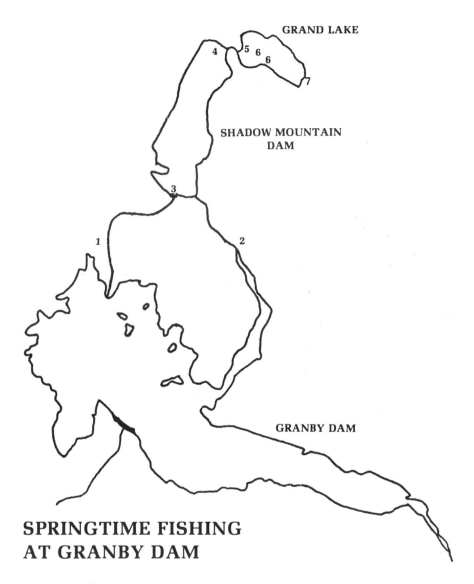

SPRINGTIME FISHING
AT GRANBY DAM

LOCATIONS

1-Pump Canal-Granby.
2-Shadow Mtn. Outlet-Colorado River Inlet to Granby
3-Shadow Mtn. Pumping Canal Inlet
4-Inlet to Shadow Mtn. at auto bridge
5-Outlet of Grand Lake at walk bridge
6-Boat fishing on Grand Lake
7-Inlet to Grand Lake

Chart II

This chart lists baits to use in specific locations (1 through 7).

TYPE OF BAIT TO USE

a–Worms/Crawlers
b–Salmon Eggs
c–Marshmallows/Cheese
d–Sucker Meat
e–Jiggs tipped with Sucker Meat
f–Trolling Gear
g–Spinning Gear
h–Nymphs

Note: Locations are identical to Chart I.

Type of Bait to Use

Locations	a	b	c	d	e	f	g	h
1	●	●	●				●	
2	●	●	●				●	●
3	●	●	●					
4	●	●	●					
5	●	●	●	●			●	
6	●			●	●	●	●	
7	●	●	●	●				

Note that under early spring conditions Granby Dam is under an unsafe and unstable ice cover. The fishing is primarily in Grand Lake, Shadow Mountain Dam, and their tributaries.

At locations 1, 4, 5, and 7, you can expect to catch a limit of small trout (eight to twelve inches) primarily by using conventional bait methods. At location 3, larger fish are the rule, especially when the Granby pump canal is pumping (usually in the very early morning hours). Location 2, is where the Colorado River flows out of Shadow Mountain Dam into Granby Dam. In this area be sure to rig properly, Browns of over fourteen pounds have been caught here. Additionally, large lake trout (Mackinaw) have been caught one mile downstream where the ripples break into the deep water of Columbine Bay at Granby Dam. Area number 6 is for boaters. Primary methods used at this time of year are trolling plugs (e.g., Rapalas, Rebels), still fishing, or open water jigging—the prey includes large Mackinaw and rainbow, plus smaller cutthroat and kokanee salmon.

Hot spots, as listed in Charts I and II for Shadow Mountain Dam and Grand Lake exist year round throughout the various seasons. The following charts feature Granby Dam and its year round hot spots.

SPRING, SUMMER, & FALL FISHING AT GRANBY DAM

LOCATIONS

8–Bay at Roaring Fork Campground
9–Arapaho Bay Flats
10–Arapaho Bay
11–Arapaho Bay
12–Dike #3
13–Main Dam
14–Rainbow Bay
15–Pump House
16–Shelter Cove
17–Columbine Bay
18–Colorado River Inlet

Chart III

This chart features spring, summer, and fall fishing at Granby Dam from ice out to ice in.

Locations

	8	9	10	11	12	13	14	15	16	17	18
A	●			●	●	●	●		●	●	●
B	●	●			●	●			●	●	●
C											
D											●
E	●		●		●	●		●	●	●	●
F				●		●					●

Type of Trout/Salmon Caught

**TYPE OF TROUT/
SALMON CAUGHT**

A–Rainbow
B–Brown
C–Brook
D–Cutthroat
E–Lake Trout
F–Kokanee Salmon

Open water fishing at Granby Dam is really a mixed bag. The successful fisherman must move from the inlets in spring to areas on the main lake to maintain quality fishing and then back to the inlets in the fall. Locations 8, 10, 16, and 17 are excellent spring and fall areas to fish, whereas, 9, 11, 13, and 15 are best fished in the hot summer months. Areas 12, 14, and 18 are above average year round. Trophy macks can be caught from the shore areas between locations 12 and 13, especially around Inspiration Point. Area 9 and 18 are hot spots for large brown trout at night on streamer flies.

Chart IV

This chart lists baits to use in specific locations (8 through 18).

Note: Locations are identical to Chart III.

TYPE OF BAIT TO USE

a–Worms/Crawlers
b–Salmon Eggs
c–Marshmallows/Cheese
d–Sucker Meat
e–Jiggs tipped with Sucker Meat
f–Trolling Gear
g–Spinning Gear
h–Flies

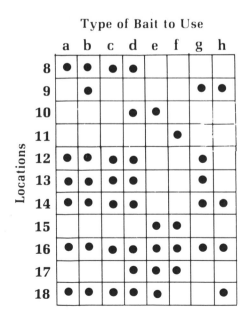

Type of Bait to Use

Locations	a	b	c	d	e	f	g	h
8	●	●	●	●				
9		●					●	●
10				●	●			
11						●		
12	●	●	●	●			●	
13	●	●	●	●			●	
14	●	●	●	●			●	●
15					●	●		
16	●	●	●	●	●	●	●	●
17				●	●	●		
18	●	●	●	●	●			●

WINTERTIME FISHING
AT GRANBY DAM

LOCATIONS

19–Arapaho Bay
20–Inspiration Point
21–Dike #3
22–Main Dam
23–Pump House
24–Elephant Island
25–Shelter Cove
26–Harvey Island
27–Columbine Bay

Winter Fishing at Granby Dam

Chart V

Chart V illustrates wintertime or ice on fishing at Granby Dam.

TYPE OF TROUT/ SALMON CAUGHT

A–Rainbow
B–Brown
C–Brook
D–Cutthroat
E–Lake Trout
F–Kokanee Salmon

Locations

Type of Trout / Salmon Caught	19	20	21	22	23	24	25	26	27
A			●		●		●		
B									
C									
D									
E	●	●	●		●	●	●	●	●
F									

Chart VI

Note: Locations are identical to Chart V.

TYPE OF BAIT TO USE

a–Worms/Crawlers
b–Salmon Eggs
c–Marshmallows/Cheese
d–Sucker Meat
e–Jiggs tipped with Sucker Meat
f–Trolling Gear
g–Flies

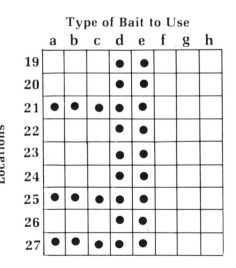

Type of Bait to Use

Locations	a	b	c	d	e	f	g	h
19				●	●			
20				●	●			
21	●	●	●	●	●			
22				●	●			
23				●	●			
24				●	●			
25	●	●	●	●	●			
26				●	●			
27	●	●	●	●	●			

The locations and methods indicated by Charts V and VI will surely creel you a wall hanging lake trout. Pay careful attention to the methods and techniques used for both jigging and baiting these behemoths. All locations are superb for lake trout. Other trout can also be caught in locations 21, 25, and 27 using more traditional methods of trout fishing.

The following text relates to the spectacular flyfishing for brown trout at Granby Dam. Many years ago, my father had taught me the secret of catching large brown trout with spinning gear. The old bubble and fly trick, except that we had a twist! I would guess that above 95 percent of the fishermen who use this method find their results as less than spectacular, but nevertheless they take some fish. This is simply because they put the fly or flies at the terminal end of the leader. This method sounds good, but consider this—the first thing that passes the fish is the bubble, not the fly.

My father and I went on one of our many weekend fishing excursions to Granby Dam and discovered the following fishing method by accident. It all kinda went like this. One of our favorite fishing places in Colorado was Granby Dam. This large impoundment had always been good to us, we consistently caught fish that ranged from ten inches to two pounds by using nightcrawlers and salmon eggs. Back then, as is the case now, Granby had a fine population of large rainbow trout and occasionally, from the bank, we would catch a kokanee salmon on hardware, such as a Super Duper or a Daredevle. Anyway...

One Friday afternoon, as we were just about to trek to this favorite impoundment, we were waylaid by a vaporlocked jeep station wagon atop Berthod Pass. That cost us about three hours and the evening fishing that was so good just before dark. We pulled into the Monarch inlet area of Granby Dam at about ten that night and were in the process of setting up our tent when an old fishy smelling critter walked up to us out of the dark. He asked us if we had any extra flashlight batteries. We accommodated him and in that great western fashion, provided him with a cup of coffee from our thermos.

We asked him if he fished any today and he said, "No, fishing at night for large brown trout is best in this lake." He told us that he had just arrived at the lake himself and was preparing to fish when his flashlight gave up the ship.

My dad was real interested in what this old man was talking about and especially in the pictures of five-pound-plus brownies. I wondered about him, he really smelled fishy. Anyway, he told us to come down to the waters edge and he would teach us "a thing or two about the habits of brownies." And off we went!

We hurriedly set up camp, grabbed our rods and bait, then walked to the waters edge. Coleman lantern in hand. He introduced himself as Ed Jano. Old Ed looked at us and our rigs in a strange manner and said, "You two really do need a teachin' about fishin'." He reached into his tackle box and pulled out a little book filled with huge flies and a couple of clear torpedo-shaped casting bubbles and proceeded to cut our lines and "rig us up properly." I thought to myself that this was weird, I'd only used bubbles (the red and white variety for sunfish and crappie and then with a worm, not with huge flies).

It looked something like this. The clear torpedo-shaped bubble was attached to the end of the line and at about eighteen inches up, Ed put a snelled fly (called a Brown Bear) and then about eighteen inches farther up he put another (called a Muddler Minnow). Ed told us that this rig was the key to some very fine fishing and that we would have to set our drags light, cast out as far as we could and then reel in very slow. Actually, he said, "very, very, very slow." So, what had we to lose—I went up the bank and Dad went with Ed.

I think that I must have casted this rig twenty times at least when I heard Ed say, "I had a tech," I think that meant that he had a hit. On the very next cast, as I reeled ultra slow daydreaming or nightdreaming, trying to locate the Big Dipper, my rod nearly was pulled out of my hands. I knew I had one and it was large.

It was about ten minutes later that I finally saw my catch, Ed turned on his flashlight and tried to net brownie, but he had other ideas, and turned tail only to strip out about twenty yards more of my line. Finally, I could feel I was winning the battle as the line came in more easily. Once more, brownie approached the bank, this time for the last time Ed cradled this fish in his net. It was the largest trout that I'd ever caught, a seven-pound eight-ounce brown trout. That night, Dad and I caught a limit each, not one was under four pounds and we had learned a fishing technique that has consistently allowed us to catch large numbers of lunker trout. Areas 8 and 9 are the locations where these fish were caught.

ELEVEN MILE RESERVOIR

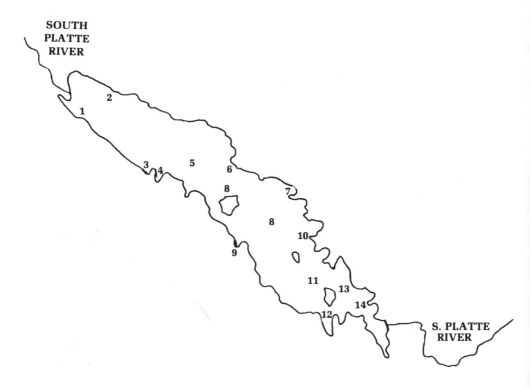

LOCATIONS

1–1st Access to Lake Near Spinney Mtn.
2–Shallow Area NE Side
3–Cove Near Boat Launch Ramp
4–2nd Access to Lake Shore
5–Mid–Lake Channel
6–Shoreline S. of Rocky Flats Campground
7–Mid–Lake NE Cove
8–Mid–Lake Channel/SE of Goose Island
9–Howbert Point
10–Walk–in Between Corral Cove & Freshwater Cove
11–Mid–Lake Channel Between Duck Is. & Deer Is.
12–Witcher's Cove
13–S. Point of East Bay Cove
14–Deep SE Cove directly Across from Witcher's Cove

2

Eleven Mile Reservoir

This reservoir is located just south of Spinney Mountain Reservoir and is part of the South Platte River drainage system. Eleven Mile Reservoir has its own claim to fame, it produced the largest kokanee salmon ever recorded during the 1985 kokanee snagging season at six pounds three ounces—this specimen is indeed large! The rainbow, browns, Mackinaw and northern pike caught in this impoundment far exceed the size of the average fish caught in similar large impoundments. The key for success, like Spinney Mountain Reservoir, is persistence.

The following map and charts are to be used together to pinpoint the best locations to fish. They are not the only locations but are locations that are proven producers.

Chart I

TYPE OF TROUT/SALMON/PIKE

A–Rainbow
B–Brown
C–Cutthroat
D–Mackinaw
E–Kokanee Salmon
F–Northern Pike

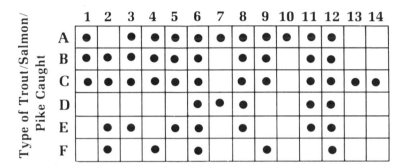

Locations

Type of Trout/Salmon/Pike Caught	1	2	3	4	5	6	7	8	9	10	11	12	13	14
A	●		●	●	●	●	●	●	●	●	●	●		
B	●	●	●	●	●	●		●	●		●	●		
C	●	●	●	●	●	●		●	●		●	●	●	●
D						●	●	●			●	●		
E		●	●		●	●		●			●	●		
F		●		●		●			●			●		

Overall, Eleven Mile Reservoir probably creels more large fish in the three pounds plus category than any other reservoir in the state. The growth rate of the fish is phenomenal, this is primarily due to a stable food chain, low level of pollution from the feeding South Platte River, and close management by the Colorado Division of Wildlife. The best springtime fishing locations combine locations 1, 3, 4, 6, 7, 8, 9, 10, 12, 13, and 14. Locations 8, 10, 13, and 14 are excellent for spring, fall, and winter lake trout via jigging methods. Fish for wintertime lake trout at location 10 and you can't go wrong, the main channel nearly touches the shore at this point. Troll for kokanee at 5, 8, 10, 11, and 13, or flyfish for them in location 2. Northerns can be caught in the shallows in late June at locations 2, 3, 4, 6, 7, 9, and 12.

Chart II

Note: Locations are identical to Chart I

TYPE OF BAIT TO USE

a–Worms/Crawlers
b–Salmon Eggs
c–Marshmallows/Cheese
d–Small Salad Shrimp
e–Jiggs tipped with Sucker Meat
f–Sucker Meat
g–Trolling Gear
h–Spinning Gear
i–Streamer Flies at Night
j–Small daytime Wet/Dry Flies

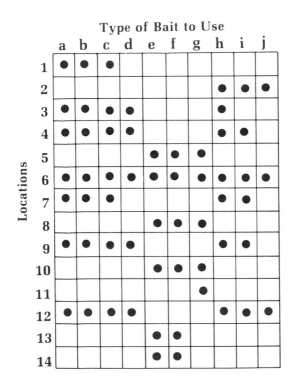

Type of Bait to Use

Locations	a	b	c	d	e	f	g	h	i	j
1	●	●	●							
2								●	●	●
3	●	●	●	●				●		
4	●	●	●	●				●	●	
5					●	●	●			
6	●	●	●	●	●	●	●	●	●	●
7	●	●	●					●	●	
8					●	●	●			
9	●	●	●	●				●	●	
10					●	●	●			
11							●			
12	●	●	●	●				●	●	●
13					●	●				
14					●	●				

Lazy winter lake near Gunnison.

Muddy Pass Lake directly above the junction of Highway 40 and 14. Contains many large trout.

3

Curecanti National Recreation Area Blue Mesa, Morrow Point, and Crystal Reservoirs

As the cool gray dawn of fall approached, a Ute named Curicata began his manhood by leaving the tribe to begin his full moon to full moon trek through the wilderness. His quest was simple, to survive in the land of his forefathers and to take his rightful place within the tribe, whatever that might be.

Curicata had prepared for this rite for the past fifteen winters. Since he was a child, his grandfather had told him of the great Wapiti who wandered from the West Elk Mountains to the great canyons surrounding the Gunnison River and the Elk Creek tributary area. Visions of this magnificent Wapiti so permeated his dreams that he felt his destiny was somehow associated with this legendary animal.

His first several moons were spent preparing rabbit snairs, honing fishing hooks from bone, and selecting from a cache of wood one branch that would make a sturdy bow. The tribe had provided him the elements to make fishing line and bow strings from—the dried intestines of a mountain ram from which catgut could be made.

On the fourth moon, he began his careful ascent into the high mesa areas seeking the shelter of the quakies (aspen) and pines. Curicata sought an area his father called "beaver meadow" where springs, creeks, meadows, and pine covered mountains all seemed to meet at once.

It was the morning following his fifteenth moon that Curicata heard the unmistakable shrill bugle of a Wapiti in a valley just over the mountain he was on. This valley was to be known as Elk Valley. As he approached the valley rim, the visions in his dreams became a reality. In a meadow not more than 500 yards away was such a magnificent elk that it made Curicata awe, its immense tines shimmered in the approaching sunlight as the legendary bull bugled a warcry to all that this was his territory.

Thoughts surfaced in Curicata's mind that a stalk through the dense pines and aspen surrounding the meadow would be difficult at best. He hungered for just one draw of the arrow at Wapiti.

For days, the stalk began the morning of each new day and lasted until the darkness invaded the forest floor. On the twenty-fifth day, Curicata began his stalk under the shadows of darkness and sat in ambush upon the trail leading into Elk Meadow. Alas, a bugle sounded to his right and was answered by another just beyond the meadow. Immediately, Wapiti raced toward the meadow, all caution aside, to engage in combat with another bull seeking his harem.

Curicata fletched an arrow from his quiver and after what seemed like an eternity, finally saw Wapiti approaching the meadow only twenty yards away. Just as this magnificent elk paused to bugle one more time, Curicata drew full draw and felled this magnificent animal. He had now become a legend in his own time.

Curicata eventually became a Ute chief. On April 11, 1956, the National Park Service named Curecanti

National Recreational Area in his honor. The initial development of this national recreational area included the Wayne Aspinal Project which proposed the building of three dams by the Bureau of Reclamation. In December 1965 Blue Mesa Dam was completed, followed by Morrow Point Dam in December 1970, and Crystal Dam in August 1976.

Blue Mesa is the largest reservoir built in the state of Colorado offering over ninety-six miles of shoreline and boasting 9,180 surface acres with a total storage capacity of 940,000-acre feet. It is primarily a water storage reservoir. Morrow Point Dam is recognized nationally as the first double curvature arch dam in the United States. That is, the dam curves from top to bottom and side to side. It contains 817 surface acres, 117,000-acre feet of storage capacity, and is used primarily as a power generating facility. Crystal Dam, the smallest of the three reservoirs contains 301 surface acres, 26,000-acre feet of storage capacity, and is primarily used to maintain an even river flow downstream into the Black Canyon of the Gunnison.

National Park Service statistics point out that over one million visitors annually enjoy the beauty of this recreation area. The primary sports relate to fishing, boating, and big game hunting. It's interesting to note that big game hunting is allowed by the National Park Service in its recreation areas but not within national park designations. For those visitors from out of state, Curecanti National Recreation Area offers a wealth of diversities centered on nature and administered from their large Visitor Center at Elk Creek.

Primary trout fishing activities center around Blue Mesa Dam, due to its accessibility. Morrow Point Dam offers prime walk in fishing only via Pine Creek Trail. Crystal Dam is nearly inaccessible except for those visitors who experience this backcountry via the concessionaire who operates private boat excursions on both Morrow Point and Crystal.

The following will focus on Blue Mesa Reservoir, the prime locations to fish for trout, and the bait most likely to creel a limit. Chart I when used in conjunction with the map will define the most productive areas of the reservoir to fish and the type of trout or salmon to expect. Chart II indicates the type of bait to use at each location in Chart I.

Chart I

Locations

Type of Trout/ Salmon Caught	1	2	3	4	5	6	7	8	9	10	11	12
A	●	●	●	●	●	●	●	●	●	●	●	●
B	●	●	●		●	●	●	●		●	●	●
C						●					●	●
D	●			●		●	●	●	●		●	

TYPE OF TROUT/ SALMON CAUGHT

A-Rainbow
B-Brown
C-Mackinaw
D-Kokanee Salmon

22

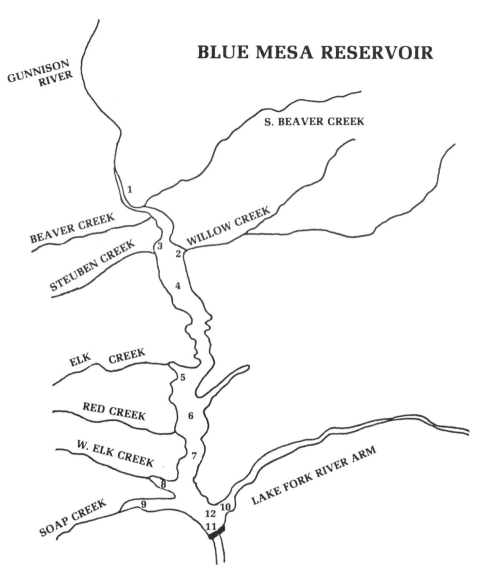

BLUE MESA RESERVOIR

GUNNISON RIVER

S. BEAVER CREEK

BEAVER CREEK

STEUBEN CREEK

WILLOW CREEK

ELK CREEK

RED CREEK

W. ELK CREEK

SOAP CREEK

LAKE FORK RIVER ARM

LOCATIONS

1-Lake City Bridge
2-Willow Creek at Iola Inlet
3-Cove above Steuben Creek
4-Mid-Lake between Steuben
& Elk Creek
5-Elk Creek
6-Mid-Lake between Elk
Creek & Red Creek

7-Mid-Lake between Red Creek
& W. Elk Creek
8-West Elk Creek Cove
9-Soap Creek Inlet
10-Lake Fork Arm Inlet at Main
Lake Near Dam
11-Dam
12-Main Channel Sapinero Basin

Chart II

Note: Locations are identical to Chart I

Type of Bait to Use

Locations	a	b	c	d	e	f	g	h	i	j
1	●	●						●	●	
2	●	●	●					●	●	
3								●	●	
4							●			
5	●	●	●	●			●			
6					●	●	●			
7							●			
8	●	●	●	●						
9	●	●	●	●						
10	●	●	●				●	●	●	
11	●	●	●	●	●	●	●	●	●	●
12					●	●	●	●	●	●

TYPE OF BAIT TO USE

a–Worms/Crawlers
b–Salmon Eggs
c–Marshmallows/Cheese
d–Small Salad Shrimp
e–Jiggs tipped with Sucker Meat
f–Sucker Meat
g–Trolling Gear
h–Spinning Gear
i–Streamer Flies at Night
j–Weighted Marabou Black Jig

Rainbows and browns are the predominant species of trout found in this reservoir and can be readily caught at the listed locations. Lake trout or Mackinaw roam the depths to the tune of 30-pounders and are generally caught in the late fall, winter, and early spring. Their downfall usually relates to their fondness with jigs tipped with sucker meat or baits composed of whole dead suckers. The kokanee salmon can be caught in several ways on flies from the bank at night, trolling, or by the use of snagging methods. During the kokanee salmon snagging season it is common to catch forty fish in a day that weigh between two and three pounds each. An interesting note to those who venture into Morrow Point Dam—in 1975 this waterway was stocked with coho (silver) salmon. Their success or failure is yet to be determined due to the lack of fishing pressure on this reservoir and its inaccessibility.

Lunker Lake near Kremmling, Colorado. Inquire at
Fishin' Hole Sporting Goods, Kremmling.

4

Spinney Mountain Reservoir

Spinney Mountain Reservoir (pronounced like a spinning rod) has probably received more press in the past three years than any other lake in the state regarding its unusually large trout. Changing regulations are the rule here—currently, you may keep only one trout of at least twenty inches or more. Additionally, the reservoir is restricted to flies and lures only and fishing is allowed from dawn to dusk.

These regulations were brought about because of the intense fishing pressure, large creel take, and the inability of a lake of this stature to be maintained as a quality fishery. I tip my hat to the Colorado Division of Wildlife for this effort.

Fishing at Spinney is a real experience. If you enter on the boat launch side, you may not be able to cross the dam unless the gates are open and then it is only one way. When the gates are open, no one seems to care which way you go. If you fish Spinney without a boat, I would recommend that you enter at the north end of Eleven Mile Reservoir where the road passes over the inlet and meanders directly toward the dam and adequate parking. Boating can be extremely hazardous because of the extreme winds and the location of the boat launch facility. I've seen as many as six boats of all sizes all on the bottom near the launch ramp because they were unable to keep the waves from swamping their boats.

The benefits of fishing this impoundment far outweigh the inconveniences. Whether you fish in a boat or on shore, your chances of success are excellent. Persistence is the key.

The following map and chart are to be used together to pinpoint the best locations to fish. Since this reservoir is limited to flies and lures only, it is not necessary to chart the various baits to use, except that you may use as an artificial bait, Lucky Lou's Artificial Salmon Eggs. Best spoons to use are Crocodiles, Kastmasters, and a #506 Super Duper. Plugs such as count down Rapalas are effective when trolling or casting from shore. Trolling Zonkers and Black Wooley Worms are effective too.

Chart I

TYPE OF TROUT/SALMON CAUGHT

A-Rainbow
B-Brown
C-Cutthroat
D-Kokanee Salmon
E-Northern Pike

Locations — Type of Trout/Salmon/Pike Caught

	1	2	3	4	5	6	7	8	9
A	●	●	●	●	●	●	●	●	
B	●	●	●	●	●	●	●	●	
C	●	●	●	●	●	●	●	●	
D	●					●		●	
E			●	●					●

SPINNEY MOUNTAIN RESERVOIR

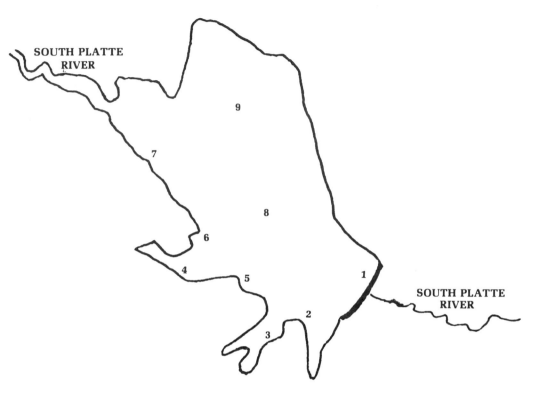

LOCATIONS

1–South Area of Dam near Launch Ramp
2–Outer Picnic Area between 1st Cove & Dam
3–2nd Southwest Cove
4–Mid–Lake Cove
5–Point between 3 & 4 above
6–Eastern Most Point where Mid–Lake Cove Ends
7–Area between South Platte Inlet to 6 above
8–Mid–Lake Channel

Areas 3, 4, and 9 are recommended for northern pike, lures and large streamers are effective in the shallows in these areas. Areas 1, 2, 5, and 6 are excellent when using lures for trout, whereas 3 and 4 are best using fly patterns from #16 fresh water shrimp imitations to Muddler Minnows and Wooley Buggers. At area 7, use all of the above methods plus Lucky Lou's Artificial Salmon Eggs—they are dynamite.

A bog exists, similar to quicksand, between areas 4 & 6, so be cautious if you are walking the shore line. Area 8 which references the main lake channel is best for trolling for trophy kokanee and the various species of trout. The state record kokanee (angling) came out of Spinney in September 1986, it was six pounds thirteen ounces.

5

Dillon Reservoir

Twilight Beckons The Stars Above

A cool mountain breeze flows down upon the mountains and permeates the forest floor as twilight beckons to the stars approaching. The sounds of a rushing river seem to permeate the air as it casually works its way into a mighty reservoir. Serenity characterizes this body of water and is only interrupted by the serenades of the owls, ducks, and the buzzing of insects. But what is the sound of the zing-zap-plop, zing-plop that curiously inhabits the inlets and bays of this waterway?

A night fly fisherman—what else? Lake Dillon in the Colorado mountains seems to have spawned a collection of unusual specimens. The typical fisherman who inhabits this realm seeks the shadows of nightfall to avoid laughter by his fellow man and to satisfy his craving for large brown trout. Can you imagine this new breed decked out with chest waders that sag one foot at the crotch (made for professional basketball players), two spinning rods, flashlights, a long handled net, mosquito lotion, a variety of fly hooks hanging from a fishing vest and to top it off, a portable radio firmly attached to the suspenders of the waders.

You've probably noticed that fishermen on any given lake usually fish to nightfall and then pack it up until the light of morning. I want to relate a trip that took place at Dillon Reservoir where the fisherman I encountered all stated that "the fishing at this lake is just terrible, it's just not the way it used to be!"

On a Friday afternoon in August, my wife, Mary, packed up the kids, while I packed up the truck for an annual camping outing with about fifteen other families that we were to meet at the lake. An hour and one-half later we arrived at our rendezvous site and began setting up camp. The first order of business was a relaxing dinner and some fellowship. About 6:00 P.M., the guys rustled up about a cord of wood for the campfire while the gals built a fire pit to contain it. As twilight approached, I began to get itchy, knowing that brown trout of immense proportions inhabited this lake.

Cautiously and calmly, I brought up the subject of fishing and generated some interest—but was somewhat surprised when no one wanted to join me in this endeavor. Probably because it would be nearly dark by the time we hiked through a tree stand to the lake. So, off I went with my baggy waders and all, while the group generally hee-hawed me. I said to Mary, "Don't worry about me, I'll be back soon!" She knew that meant hours.

As I trod my way through the trees toward the lakeshore, I was surprised to see a four-point buck in velvet. He looked at me as if I was something never seen before. Must have been the portable radio! As I approached the lake, I studied it for several minutes since it was an area I'd never fished before. The lake basically has a mud, sand, and rock bottom except for some bushy shallow bays. Studying the shoreline allowed me to see where a kind of swampy area existed. Tall grass could be seen poking through the water, as well as brush thickets. That was what I was looking for! I carefully trudged forward close to the shoreline into the heart of this bay until I saw a fish dimple the water.

This place was rather awkward, I couldn't put down the other fishing pole on the bank because it was some twenty yards into the marsh, so I stuffed it into my waders—making it look like an antennae. This must have scared the other fishermen away because no others were in sight.

Many years before, my father had taught me the secret of catching large brown trout with spinning gear. The old bubble and fly trick, except that we had a twist! I would guess that well above 95 percent of the fishermen who use this method find their results as less than spectacular, but nevertheless they take some fish. This is simply because they put the fly or flies at the terminal end of the leader. This method sounds good, but consider this—the first thing that passes the fish is the bubble, not the fly. Out of the dozens of fish I caught and released that weekend, only two were caught on an experimental leader added to the end of the bubble. Additionally, all of the fish kept were over two pounds.

The end result to this story was that as I wandered back into camp, it got real quiet, I think I scared them. Anyway, when they saw the unusually large fish I was hefting, they began to question me in detail how I did it.

I'm going to fill you in on how I did it—and you can too—but first I want to give you some information about this unique reservoir. Lake Dillon is a large 3200-acre reservoir surrounded by the new city of Dillon on the north and "old" Frisco at the south. Old Dillon resides some sixty to eighty feet under the surface of the water.

In 1959, the Denver Water Board began construction on Dillon Reservoir and the Roberts Tunnel (which would carry the water from Dillon to Denver). The Roberts Tunnel was completed in 1962, while the construction of the reservoir seemed to hit one snag after the other, such as: relocation or abandonment of old Dillon; the relocation of thirteen miles of highway, eight miles of transmission line, a hydroelectric plant, a forest service station, and the old Dillon cemetery. Dillon Reservoir was completed in 1963 and now boasts 26.8 miles of shoreline and a water carrying capacity of 254,000-acre feet of storage.

Modern maps of the lake distinctly show the old paved roads, which now are used as launch ramps, but used to go through the heart of old Dillon. Old Dillon residents were allowed to stay in their homes until the reservoir was nearly completed—then a choice had to be exercised. The Denver Water Board would buy the property at fair market value, relocate structures to a small town called Silverthorn, or offer the residents parcels of the new Dillon which was then under construction.

The cities of Dillon, Silverthorn, and Frisco are now known far and wide for the recreational diversity that now exists in this scenic area. Names like Breckenridge, Keystone, and Copper Mountain ski resorts are familiar in recreational circles coast-to-coast. Dillon Reservoir has also received national recognition for its fine fishing—most recently through the nationally syndicated radio show called the "In Fisherman" (March 28 & 30, 1988). The director of this show, Brooke Snavely, spoke of brown trout fishing beyond the imagination and a comment on fishing "with the likes of Merton Leeper."

Now, for the proper methods and techniques. Anyone trout fishing in Colorado can catch a fish on flies either with a flyrod or a spinning rod. A flyrod combination

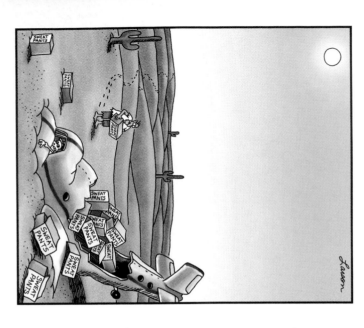

The Far Side®

LAST IMPRESSIONS

— 2002 —

July

Monday 1

Canada Day

allows the user the advantage of floating lines that keep the fly on top or sinking lines that keep the fly just below the surface. The purist fly fisherman is sure that the use of these combinations is the only way to fly fish. Spinning rods equipped with a bubble and a fly can cover more water and in my opinion catch more fish, at least, in lakes. The natural action of the floating or sinking fly line in a river is another matter—the purist fly fisherman wins hands down.

The flyrod, reel, and line are self-explanatory, but the spinning rod fly outfit isn't. Use no heavier than 8-pound text monofilament, 6-pound is probably the best. Attach a torpedo-shaped clear bubble (float) and one or two flies. Two methods are commonly used by spin fishermen, they are: (1) to attach the bubble about three feet above the fly or (2) to attach the bubble to the terminal end of the line and put a fly three feet above the bubble. Note the following example.

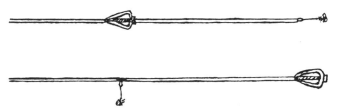

I use both of these methods at once by using a product called "AdjustaBubble." This float allows my line to go through a seated chamber and attach to the line anywhere I want without any knots in my line. It looks something like the following illustration:

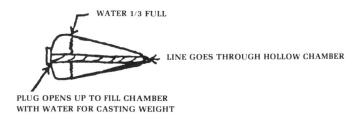

WATER 1/3 FULL

LINE GOES THROUGH HOLLOW CHAMBER

PLUG OPENS UP TO FILL CHAMBER
WITH WATER FOR CASTING WEIGHT

My fly fishing outfit looks like this.

Now for the technique and problem analysis. Which fly do you think catches the most fish? Most people would answer, the bottom fly—but the top fly above the bubble is actually the most productive. The reason, I believe, is because it passes the fish first and is not disturbed by any kind of bubble wake.

The flies used and the time of day on a twenty-four hour clock, directly affect the creel take. For instance, in light hours, I use reasonably small flies such as a female Black Gnat, a Mosquito or a mini Muddler Minnow. If I could only afford three small flies I would use a Black Gnat, Adams and a Renegade. In the darkened hours though, when the moon is not present or very small, I use large flies attached to #2, #4, and #6 hooks. My all-time favorite is the Muddler Minnow, with the Brown Bear, Zonker, Hornberg, and Black Wooley Worm in close contention.

The technique, day or night, is to cast out as far as you can and retrieve your flies very, very slowly. I always keep my index finger and thumb together around the rod in front of the reel, this allows the line to pass through my fingers enabling one to defect the slightest strike. Patience is the fly fisherman's forte, if you are persistent and don't give up, I guarantee you will put fish on your stringer.

Flyfishing at night is the only consistent way that I know of catching lunker trout time after time. When fishing at night I am very particular about the way I tie my flies on, I don't just loop them on, but tie a blood dropper. This knot is just about a 100 percent knot, in other words, my 8-pound test line will not be weakened at the point of the knot. The blood dropper is used to tie a loop into your line above the bubble or below your bubble for a two-fly setup.

Blood Dropper Knot

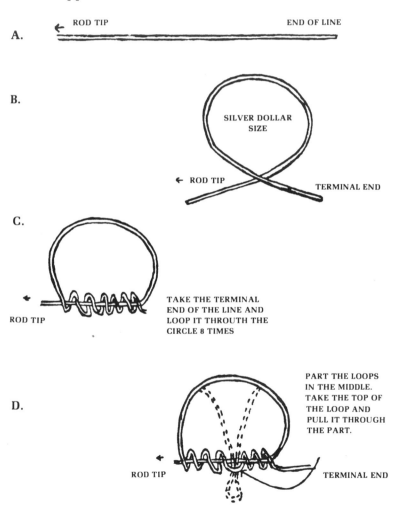

E.

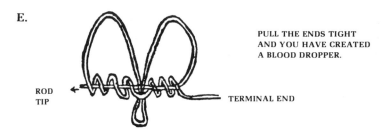

PULL THE ENDS TIGHT
AND YOU HAVE CREATED
A BLOOD DROPPER.

ROD
TIP

TERMINAL END

F.

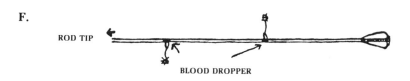

ROD TIP

BLOOD DROPPER

Another advantage to this knot is that it sits straight out from the monofilament and does not parallel the line up or down, thus, your fly tends to stay away from tangles on your line. Now for the fly.

Buying snelled flies used to be no problem in Colorado —they were always available—not now though, I have seen very few in the last ten years. So, now we must snell our own and this is how. Use 12-pound test line for the snell, it is rigid enough to stay away from your line and avoids tangles. Simply tie an improved clench knot on the eye of the fly and then tie it or loop it onto your blood dropper.

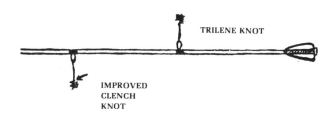

TRILENE KNOT

IMPROVED
CLENCH
KNOT

Another excellent knot to use to snell flies is the trilene knot. It is probably superior in strength to the improved clench knot and is easy to tie.

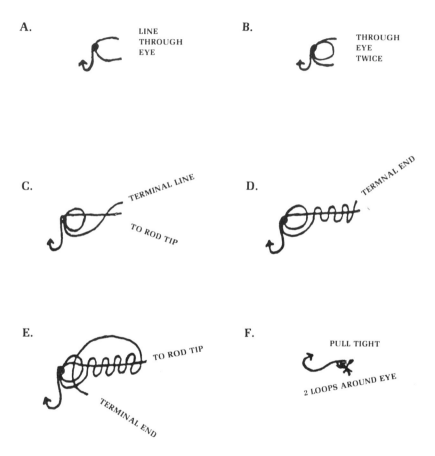

A. LINE THROUGH EYE

B. THROUGH EYE TWICE

C. TERMINAL LINE / TO ROD TIP

D. TERMINAL END

E. TO ROD TIP / TERMINAL END

F. PULL TIGHT / 2 LOOPS AROUND EYE

Note that if you choose to loop your fly onto your blood dropper, you need to put the line loop through your snelled hook loop to create a square knot. Doing it any other way will weaken this conjunction.

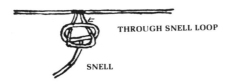

THROUGH SNELL LOOP

SNELL

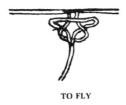

TO FLY

When you try night fishing in this manner, I suggest you try the area at Dillon Dam, near Frisco where the Blue River runs into the reservoir. You will need waders and a good flashlight. Cast into this area just where the current seems to end and it becomes calmer. Crank ever so slowly and be patient. I have often thrown flies for over ninety minutes without a strike and then gotten strikes every cast after that for hours.

When trying this technique, keep a log on the numbers of fish caught above and below the bubble. you will soon note that the scales are tipped heavily toward those flies above the bubble. For several years now, my bubble resides at the terminal end of my line and my flies are arranged upward toward my rod tip. This is the recommended method to use for success!

One last tip to remember about night fly fishing is, when the moon is out and bright upon the water—go to bed and rest, the fish just don't hit flies. And never take a lantern near the waters edge, it spooks the fish and severely limits your success. Shield it from the water and place it far onto the bank.

Dillon Reservoir. Mert with flyrod in hand. Fish caught at the
Blue River Inlet.

The following illustrations will map the shoreline of the reservoir, chart the best places to fish, and recommend the technique to use at each location cites.

Chart I

TYPE OF TROUT/
SALMON CAUGHT

A–Rainbow
B–Brown
C–Brook
D–Cutthroat
E–Kokanee Salmon
F–Coho Salmon
G–Chinook Salmon
H–Arctic Char
    To be stocked in Fall 1988

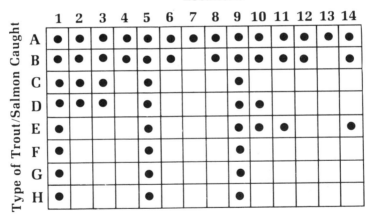

Locations

Type of Trout/Salmon Caught	1	2	3	4	5	6	7	8	9	10	11	12	13	14
A	●	●	●	●	●	●	●	●	●	●	●	●	●	●
B	●	●	●	●	●	●		●	●	●	●	●		●
C	●	●	●		●				●					
D	●	●	●		●				●	●				
E	●				●				●	●	●			●
F	●				●				●					
G	●				●				●					
H	●				●				●					

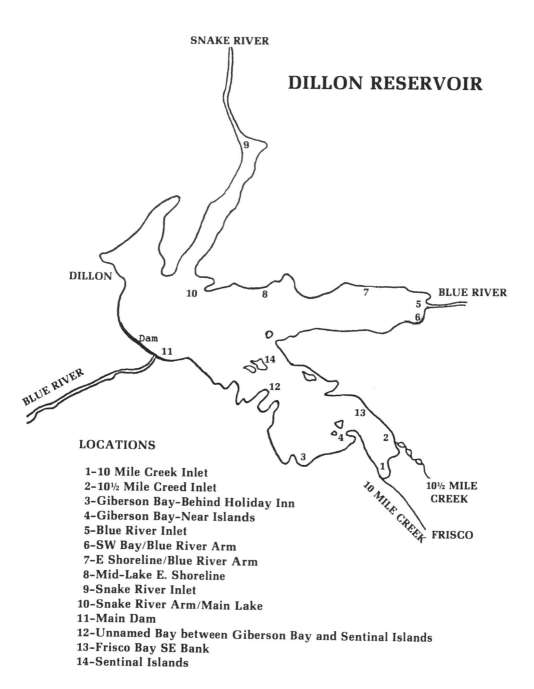

DILLON RESERVOIR

SNAKE RIVER

DILLON

BLUE RIVER

BLUE RIVER

Dam

10½ MILE CREEK

10 MILE CREEK

FRISCO

LOCATIONS

1-10 Mile Creek Inlet
2-10½ Mile Creed Inlet
3-Giberson Bay-Behind Holiday Inn
4-Giberson Bay-Near Islands
5-Blue River Inlet
6-SW Bay/Blue River Arm
7-E Shoreline/Blue River Arm
8-Mid-Lake E. Shoreline
9-Snake River Inlet
10-Snake River Arm/Main Lake
11-Main Dam
12-Unnamed Bay between Giberson Bay and Sentinal Islands
13-Frisco Bay SE Bank
14-Sentinal Islands

Chart II

Note: Locations are identical to Chart I

TYPE OF BAIT TO USE

a–Worms/Crawlers
b–Salmon Eggs
c–Marshmallows/Cheese
d–Jiggs tipped with Meal Worms
e–Trolling Gear
f–Spinning Gear
g–Flies

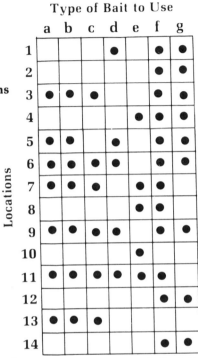

Type of Bait to Use

Locations	a	b	c	d	e	f	g
1				●		●	●
2						●	●
3	●	●	●			●	●
4					●	●	●
5	●	●		●		●	●
6	●	●	●	●		●	●
7	●	●	●			●	●
8						●	●
9	●	●	●	●		●	●
10						●	
11	●	●	●	●	●	●	
12						●	●
13	●	●	●				
14						●	●

The best early springtime locations are areas 1, 2, 5, 7, 9, and 11. Do not begin fishing areas, 1, 2, 3, 5, or 9 until New Moon closest to the end of May or the first two weeks in June if using flies. Trolling is best in areas 7, 8, 10, 11, 12, and 14. Snagging for kokanee is best in areas 9 and 11. Overall, this reservoir is one of the best producers of brown trout in the state and the key to catching them is to fish only at night when no moon is present and to use Rapalas or Streamer Flies, such as, the Brown Bear, Muddler Minnow, Zonker, or Black Wooley Worm with a red feather tail. Wintertime fishing is productive at areas 1, 5, 6, 9, and 11 using small jigs tipped with meal worms.

6

Green Mountain Dam

The mountains and lush green valleys that surround this impoundment contain some of the best big game hunting in the state for deer and elk. Likewise, this 2,125-acre reservoir contains a wealth of fishing opportunities for both the trophy angler and the pleasure angler. This reservoir is often passed up by many anglers due to novel and unique conditions that exist year after year.

In the late fall, this impoundment is lowered to almost half of its carrying capacity, due to the tremendous yearly runoff it receives. Thus, the serious trout angler normally seeks stable water levels which fully maintain the ecological food balance so necessary for trout to survive. This particular waterway seems to disregard stated ecological facts and continues year-after-year to produce an incredible number of trout and kokanee salmon for the angler.

Lake trout, (Mackinaw) are rarely seriously fished for, even though a thirty-pounder was caught on a night crawler in 1987. The kokanee salmon population staggers the imagination, in terms of sheer numbers and the moderate size of the four-year-old fish. Rainbow trout are most commonly caught here, creel census checks disclose that they average twelve inches in length. The brown trout is somewhat elusive and seriously fished for very little—many trophy browns exist here. Some of the smaller inlets, such as Cataract Creek often surprise the angler with a brook trout or two in the ten- to twelve-inch category.

The following map and corresponding charts primarily relate to the seasons of spring, summer, and fall. The best areas to fish are identified by the indicated locations on the map. Wintertime fishing can be hazardous, due to the tremendous water level fluctuations of this reservoir. For example, how would you feel if you spent a lot of time hiking out to a good area in the middle of the lake, augered an ice hole and found that you were walking on the first sheet of ice and that the second (and most stable ice) was three feet below your auger hole? Use caution when ice fishing and utilize the spring, summer, and fall locations for the best angling.

Chart I

TYPE OF TROUT/SALMON CAUGHT

A–Rainbow
B–Brown
C–Brook
D–Lake Trout
E–Kokanee Salmon

Locations

Type of Trout/Salmon Caught	1	2	3	4	5	6	7	8	9	10
A	●	●		●	●		●	●	●	●
B	●			●	●	●	●	●	●	●
C					●					
D					●	●	●			
E	●		●			●		●		

GREEN MOUNTAIN RESERVOIR

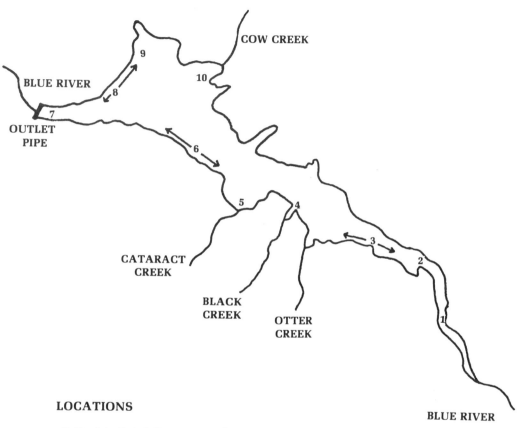

COW CREEK

9

BLUE RIVER

10

8

7

OUTLET
PIPE

6

5

4

CATARACT
CREEK

3

2

BLACK
CREEK

OTTER
CREEK

1

BLUE RIVER

LOCATIONS

1-Prairie Point Campground
2-Directly across from McDonald Flats Campground
3-In front and Northwest of McDonald Flats Campground
4-Black Creek Inlet
5-Cataract Creek Inlet
6-Southwest Bank-Spanning from Cataract Creek Camp to Heeney
7-Outlet Pipe Near Dam
8-Southwest of Willows Camp
9-Willows Campground
10-Cow Creek Camp Area

Chart II

This chart lists baits to use in specific locations (1 through 10).

Note: Locations are identical to Chart I

TYPE OF BAIT TO USE

a–Worms/Crawlers
b–Salmon Eggs
c–Marshmallows/Cheese
d–Sucker Meat
e–Jiggs tipped with Sucker Meat
f–Trolling Gear
g–Spinning Gear
h–Flies

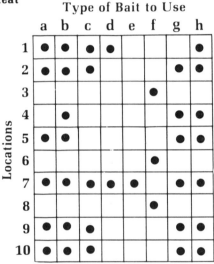

Type of Bait to Use

Locations	a	b	c	d	e	f	g	h
1	●	●	●	●				●
2	●	●	●				●	●
3					●			
4		●					●	●
5	●	●					●	●
6						●		
7	●	●	●	●	●		●	●
8						●		
9	●	●	●				●	●
10	●	●	●				●	●

The best early springtime locations are areas 7 and 9. For trolling 6 and 8 are tops until the reservoir fills, then concentrate on areas 3 and 6. Early summer through fall provides the best overall fishing opportunities at locations 1, 2, 3, 5, and 9. The kokanee salmon fall snagging season is hard to beat at areas 1 and 2. For those anglers interested in the "Big Macks," area 7 is tops for sucker meat baits from the bank and open water jigging from a boat.

7

Lake John, North, South, and East Delaney Buttes

These popular North Park lakes are found just ten miles west of the town of Walden. Lake John and the Delaney Buttes are situated amidst a background of sagebrush, meadows, meandering rivers and streams which dot the landscape and soon give way to the aspen and pines of the surrounding high country.

These lakes have a unique history. In the late fifties and early sixties, these lakes were utilized as brood lakes, whereby, the trout eggs were used to stock other lakes and river systems throughout this region. When the lakes first opened up to public fishing, it was commonplace to catch one's limit in just a few hours. The limit at this time was ten fish or ten pounds. It may as well have been less though, because creel checks disclosed that of every two or three fish caught, the weight exceeded ten pounds.

The growth rate of the trout at these lakes rival the more well known and publicized waters of Spinney and Eleven Mile dams. This is due to the tremendous numbers of fresh water shrimp that inhabit these waters.

The following maps and charts of these impoundments will clearly illustrate the most productive areas to fish.

Chart I

TYPE OF TROUT CAUGHT

A–Rainbow
B–Brook
C–Brown
D–Cutthroat

Type of Trout/Salmon Caught — Locations

	1	2	3	4	5	6	7	8	9
A	●	●	●	●	●	●	●	●	●
B	●	●	●	●	●	●	●	●	●
C	●	●				●	●	●	●
D	●	●	●	●	●		●	●	●

Chart II

Note: Locations are identical to Chart I

TYPE OF BAIT TO USE

a–Worms/Crawlers
b–Salmon Eggs
c–Marshmallows/Cheese
d–Jiggs tipped with Meal Worms
e–Trolling Gear
f–Spinning Gear
g–Streamer Flies at Night

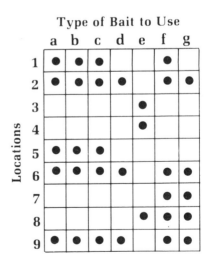

Type of Bait to Use — Locations

	a	b	c	d	e	f	g
1	●	●	●			●	
2	●	●	●	●		●	●
3					●		
4					●		
5	●	●	●				
6	●	●	●	●		●	●
7						●	●
8					●	●	●
9	●	●	●	●		●	●

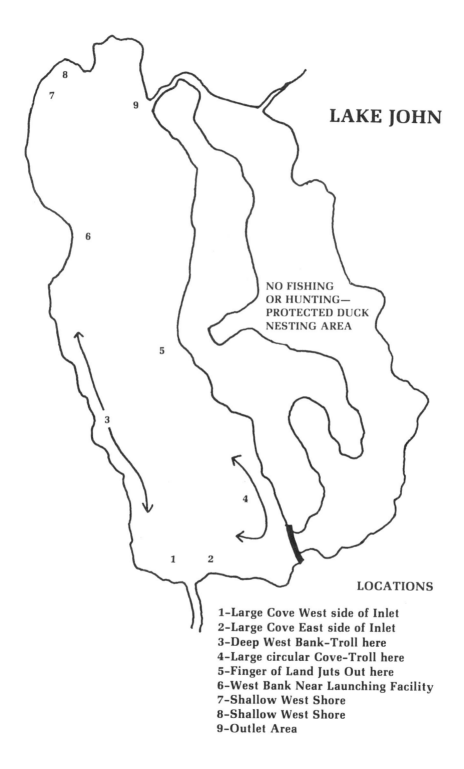

LAKE JOHN

NO FISHING
OR HUNTING—
PROTECTED DUCK
NESTING AREA

LOCATIONS

1–Large Cove West side of Inlet
2–Large Cove East side of Inlet
3–Deep West Bank–Troll here
4–Large circular Cove–Troll here
5–Finger of Land Juts Out here
6–West Bank Near Launching Facility
7–Shallow West Shore
8–Shallow West Shore
9–Outlet Area

51

Chart III

Chart III is to be used in conjunction with the Delaney Buttes lakes map on the opposite page. The locations listed are not the only places to fish these lakes, but are the most productive. Locations are defined and listed on the map as 1 through 10. The type of trout caught are listed as A through D.

TYPE OF TROUT CAUGHT

A–Rainbow
B–Brook
C–Brown
D–Cutthroat

Locations

Type of Trout/Salmon Caught	1	2	3	4	5	6	7	8	9	10
A	●	●	●	●	●	●	●	●	●	●
B	●	●	●					●	●	●
C								●	●	●
D	●	●	●	●	●	●	●	●	●	●

LOCATIONS

  1–North end of East Lake
  2–West end of East Lake (Shallows to Drop Off)
  3–Shallows, South end East Lake
  4–South Lake (Canal between Lakes)
  5–South Lake Area Just Off Frontage Road
  6–South Lake Pave Camp Area (West Shore)
  7–South Lake (Fish Between Willows)
  8–North Lake (Small Creek Inlet)
  9–North Lake Sand Bar
10–North Lake Just South of Launch Ramp

DELANEY BUTTES LAKES

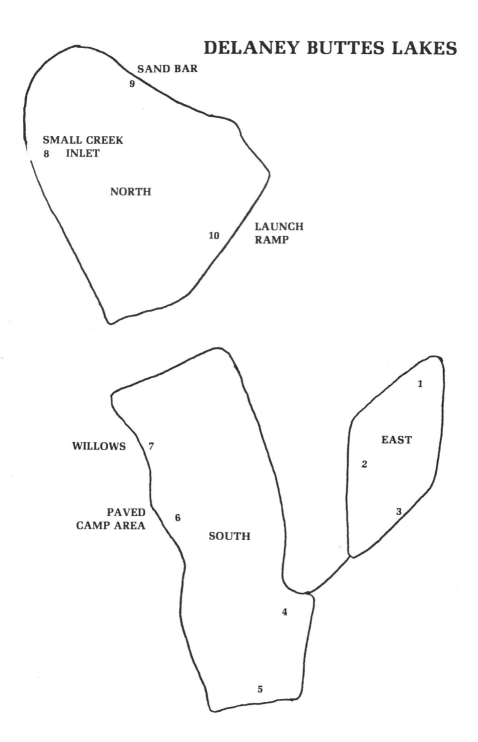

SAND BAR

9

SMALL CREEK
8   INLET

NORTH

LAUNCH
RAMP

10

1

EAST

2

WILLOWS   7

3

PAVED
CAMP AREA   6

SOUTH

4

5

Chart IV

Note: Locations are identical to Chart III

TYPE OF BAIT TO USE

a–Worms/Crawlers
b–Salmon Eggs
c–Marshmallows/Cheese
d–Jiggs tipped with Meal Worms
e–Trolling Gear
f–Spinning Gear
g–Streamer Flies at Night

Type of Bait to Use

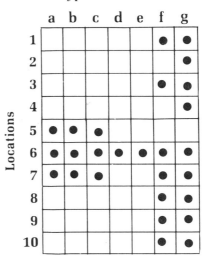

Locations	a	b	c	d	e	f	g
1						●	●
2							●
3						●	●
4							●
5	●	●	●				
6	●	●	●	●	●	●	●
7	●	●	●			●	●
8						●	●
9						●	●
10						●	●

Lake John and the Delaney Buttes lakes are shallow, thirty feet maximum in John and twenty-five in the Buttes. This factor alone creates a multitude of fish management problems. The combination of shallow depths and the large numbers of fresh water shrimp in these lakes create an astounding growth rate to the trout that inhabit these waters. The moss creates an ideal habitat for the fresh water shrimp—but also creates a higher potential for winter kill in severe winters. John's problems are compounded by the vast numbers of suckers that come into the lake via a small inlet.

Over the years, Lake John has been chemically treated, for the purpose of killing all fish (the targeted prey are the suckers and other trash fish). This factor alone restricts the overall potential of trout beyond the ten pound range. Delaney Buttes does not have the same problem associated to the trash fish because they are primarily spring fed. The major detriment to these lakes is their shallow water and the tremendous moss growth. This computes to winter kill as a reality during severe winters. Thus, it is again unlikely that fish over the ten pound class will be creeled here.

Overall though, these lakes are excellent fisheries. The average fish ranges from about one and one-half pounds to three pounds in weight. Lake John and South Delaney Butte Lake are great ice out lakes. Lures such as Super Dupers, Crocodiles, and Hammered Spoons work well at this time. Bait fishing with eggs and marsh-mallows probably creel more spring fish than any other method. Mid-summer fishing with an Adjusta-Bubble and streamer flies creel the largest and most fish of any method during these hot times. Ice fishing on Lake John is best in shallow water in locations 5, 7, 8, and 9 using euro-larvae and meal worms tipped on jugs. Ice fish South Delaney Butte Lake at location 6 using the same method.

North and East Delaney Buttes can only be fished by the use of flies and lures only. Streamer flies such as the Zonker and Brown Bear are by far the best patterns to use at night. Large brook trout can be found in numbers at the East Lake, while large brown trout are the rule at the North Lake.

STEAMBOAT LAKE

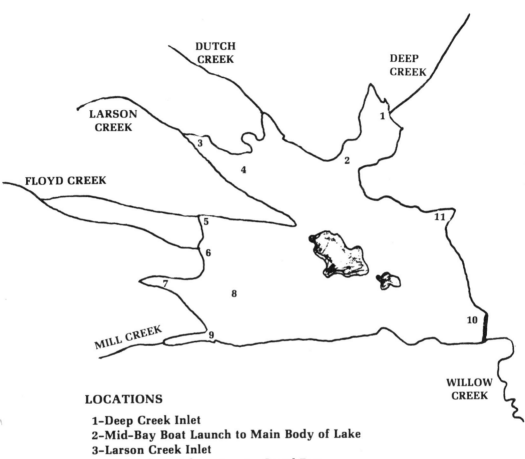

DUTCH CREEK

DEEP CREEK

LARSON CREEK

FLOYD CREEK

MILL CREEK

WILLOW CREEK

LOCATIONS

1–Deep Creek Inlet
2–Mid-Bay Boat Launch to Main Body of Lake
3–Larson Creek Inlet
4–Mid-Lake out from Larson Creed Bay
5–N. Floyd Creek Inlet
6–S. Floyd Creek Inlet
7–Meadow Point Cove
8–Mid-Lake in Front of Meadow Point
9–Mill Creek Inlet
10–Sage Flats Near Dam
11–1st Cove North of Sage Flats

Note: At all locations listed above, rainbow, brown, and cutthroat trout will be caught. Chart I lists the baits used at each location.

8

Steamboat Lake

Steamboat Lake is located directly north and just a little east of Steamboat Springs. It is approximately nineteen miles south of the Wyoming border. It is best known for its family recreational campsites and its fine fishing.

The species of fish that reside in this lake are rainbows, browns, cutthroats. Several years ago, this lake was planted with grayling which apparently did not survive. You may, at times, also catch a brookie or two when fishing near the inlets where small tributary streams empty into the lake.

Areas 1, 3, 5, and 6 are exceptional when fishing with a spinning rod equipped with a fly and bubble. These areas also excel when using the various bait methods. The fishing is so good at this lake that it is difficult to imagine an area that does not produce. The locations plotted on the map and chart are favorites of those who fish at Steamboat. They may become your favorites too.

Chart I

TYPE OF BAIT TO USE

a–Worms/Crawlers
b–Salmon Eggs
c–Marshmallows/Cheese
d–Night Time Streamer Flies
e–Hellgramites (Stone Fly)
f–Trolling Gear
g–Spinning Gear
h–Flies–Small Wet/Dry, Daytime

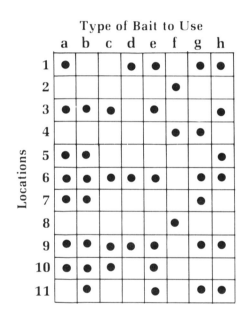

Type of Bait to Use

Locations	a	b	c	d	e	f	g	h
1	●			●	●		●	●
2						●		
3	●	●	●		●			●
4					●	●		
5	●	●						●
6	●	●	●	●	●		●	●
7	●	●					●	
8						●		
9	●	●	●	●	●		●	●
10	●	●	●		●			
11		●			●		●	●

9

Reudi Reservoir

Reudi Reservoir is located in one of the most scenic areas of Colorado, near Basalt and a part of the Fryingpan river system. Fishing activities in this area have primarily been slanted toward the river. Below Reudi, in the Fryingpan River, it is common to catch trout in excess of eight pounds in catch and release waters. The reservoir itself is often overlooked as a quality fishery and is seen by some as a put and take fishery. Not true, quality and quantity of lunker trout exist here if you fish it properly.

The average size of the trout measures ten to twelve inches in length, they are commonly stockers, and are more than cooperative. Some large trout also inhabit this waterway but have been educated to the normal crawler/egg baits and are very selective in their tablefare. A Black Wooley Worm with a red feather tail (size 6) and a Silver Zonker with gray rabbit rabbit fur (size 6) will fill your stringer with trout exceeding two pounds each, if you set up as described in chapter five.

One of the best kept secrets here is the excellent Mackinaw fishing. These trout are generally on the smallish side, eighteen to twenty inches, but they are accessible year round by jigging open water at a depth of sixty-two feet. Using a Fat Gitzit with a quarter-ounce jig head in the clear sparkle color tipped with sucker meat. My last outing netted one fish of thirty-one inches that weighed just under twelve pounds (this fish was released). We caught an additional sixteen Macks in the eighteen- to twenty-three-inch range.

Kokanee salmon also inhabit these waters and are a relatively new species for Reudi. This factor alone spells growth for the Mackinaw and the potential for a future lake trout trophy fishery.

The following map and charts of this lake should provide you with the tools you need for a most enjoyable weekend of fishing.

Chart I

TYPE OF TROUT/SALMON CAUGHT

A–Rainbow
B–Brown
C–Brook
D–Mackinaw
E–Kokanee Salmon

Locations

Type of Trout / Salmon Caught	1	2	3	4	5	6	7
A	●	●	●	●			●
B	●	●	●				●
C	●						●
D				●	●	●	
E				●	●	●	

REUDI RESERVOIR

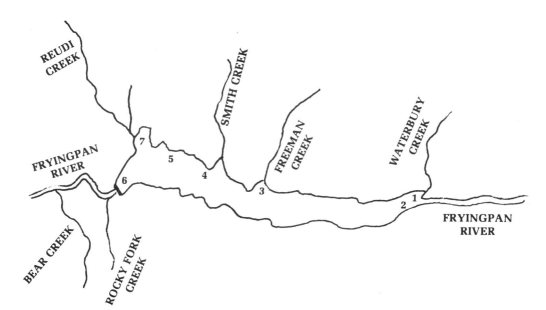

LOCATIONS

1–Waterbury Creek/Fryingpan Inlet
2–S. Shore Creek Inlet
3–Freeman Creek Inlet
4–Smith Creek Inlet
5–Between Smith Creek Inlet & Reudi Marina
6–Open Water Near Dam in 62 ft. of Water
7–Reudi Creek Inlet

Note: Locations are identical to Chart I

TYPE OF BAIT TO USE

a–Worms/Crawlers
b–Salmon Eggs
c–Marshmallows/Cheese
d–Sucker Meat
e–Jiggs tipped with Sucker Meat
f–Trolling Gear
g–Spinning Gear
h–Daytime Flies–Small/Nighttime Streamers

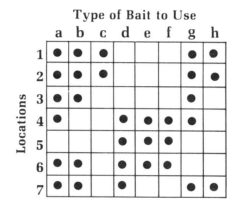

Type of Bait to Use

Locations	a	b	c	d	e	f	g	h
1	●	●	●				●	●
2	●	●	●				●	●
3	●	●					●	
4	●			●	●	●	●	
5				●	●	●		
6	●	●		●	●	●		
7	●	●		●			●	●

10

Twin Lakes

The following map and charts relate to the trout fishing at popular Twin Lakes. A brief history of this site primarily relates to the season of winter, thus, the fishing season descriptions will start with winter and transcend into the seasons of spring, summer, and fall. Note that *all* locations listed are excellent throughout the year.

Shades of dark gray clouds shelter the twilight of dawn and create an eerie mist. The air is cool, in fact, about ten degrees below zero...which is typical at Twin Lakes near Leadville, Colorado.

Twin Lakes has a unique and novel history. In the past, it was a single lake which was primarily used in winter for its commercial sales of ice. The ice was cut in blocks for use in home coolers (before modern refrigerators were in use.) Fishing in wintertime was a secondary endeavor.

With the need for domestic water needs, irrigation requirements, and the potential for the development of a quality recreational area, this single lake became two as the surrounding landscape disappeared and was engulfed with water. Thus, Twin Lakes was born. The upper lake is small, while the lower lake contains a large dam, only a waterway separates the two lakes.

Over the years, Twin Lakes has become a mecca for an unusual sort of character. Small cities literally spring up on the ice just after the ice forms. Then a few months later, they disappear as fast as they appeared. Twin Lakes is one of the few places in Colorado where ice houses are allowed as permanent winter structures. Your name, telephone number, and license must be legally displayed in contrasting colors on the outside and on the shore side of the shelter. These statistics must be at least two inches in diameter.

Locals have always boasted about the quality fishery that exists here. The primary species caught are the rainbow and brown trout. Lunker Mackinaw inhabit these lakes in vast numbers but are primarily nabbed in the area of the old lake bed or the deep water near the power house. In any event, this text will focus on the methods and techniques of ice fishing for the rainbow and brown trout.

Locating productive areas in any lake constitutes a perplexing quagmire for any fisherman—but not at Twin Lakes! Simply drill your ice hole, peer through this hole in a prone position and be prepared for a sight that will stimulate your adrenaline. You will literally see school after school of trout. The rainbow and browns will be suspended in the depths, while the Mackinaw cruise the bottom.

Rig as you would for any ice fishing endeavor, that is, a short rod (not exceeding thirty-six inches in length) and your favorite reel. Wintertime baits are unique and not characteristic of those used in the open water season of the year. Typical baits and a description of their use is as follows.

Wintertime baits generally combine with a lead headed jig hook tipped with a variety of larvae. Euro-larvae, wax worms, meal worms, and even maggots (yuk!) are some of the best wintertime larvae to use. Euro-larvae is really a tremendous and novel bait, it resembles small meal worms, except that they are colored red, white and blue, naturally. Another popular bait which is not well known is the rat-tailed maggot or better known as mouses. They look like a miniature mouse with a tail and live in water as their natural habitat.

To use larvae, simply tip a small jig with them, peer into the hole, and estimate the feet of line needed to get to the fish, then lower your line to the appropriate level and ZAP you will literally cash in on some very fine eating. Near the power plant, in about twelve to fifteen feet of water, it is more than a possibility that you'll creel your eight fish limit in little more than five minutes. So consider some catch and release on your trip to this lake.

Popular jigs that work best in Colorado water include very small Mister Twisters, Sassy Shad's, Crappie Killers, or any variety of small lead headed jugs in a soft rubber or feathered body. Preferred colors are white, chartreuse, black, and yellow. The more traditional year round baits and lures will also creel fish through the ice except that it requires the angler to make some modifications to existing equipment.

When using crawlers, red worms, salmon eggs, and marshmallows, it is necessary to attach a spring tip to your rod and to use a sliding sinker rig in order to detect the slightest strike. Remember the discussion on water phenomena and the ideal water temperatures for the various species of trout? (Found in *Colorado Trout Fishing: Methods and Techniques*.) Rainbows are most active at fifty-five degrees while browns are most active at sixty degrees, therefore, in the winter months when the subsurface water is in the forties, these fish are somewhat sluggish and attack their meal in slow motion. To feel these slight strikes it is necessary to use a spring tip. One can easily be made by taking the spring

out of an old ball point pen and straightening it: one of
the ends represents the eyelet extending about three to
four inches beyond the rod tip, while the other
represents a straight wire attached to the rod. It looks
something like this:

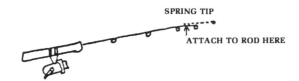

These methods can be used anywhere an ice cover
rests upon the water to locate fish. The look and see
method saves many hours of waiting for a fish to happen
by. Best areas to look for on lakes that are new to you is
on the inlet areas which appear to shallow out into drop
offs. Generally you will be able to see the fish suspended
near the deeper water and occasionally see a "monster"
come into view from the depths searching for a quick
meal and then a hasty retreat back into the dark depths.

Chart I

This chart is to be used in combination with the map of
Twin Lakes. Locations are defined and listed on the map
as 1 through 9. The type of trout are defined on the chart
as A through C.

TYPE OF TROUT CAUGHT

A–Rainbow
B–Brown
C–Lake Trout

Type of Trout / Salmon Caught		Locations								
		1	2	3	4	5	6	7	8	9
	A	●		●	●	●	●		●	●
	B	●		●	●		●		●	
	C		●		●	●		●		

TWIN LAKES

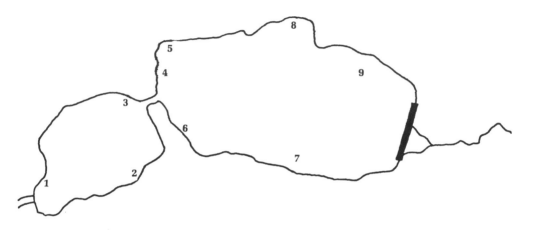

LOCATIONS

1-Upper Lake Near Inlet
2 & 3-Upper Lake
4-Lower Lake Power House Area
5-Lower Lake Rocky Area Near Power House
6-Lower Lake Near Old Ice House
7-Lower Lake Old Lake Bed
8-Lower Lake Hill Area
9-Lower Lake Area Between Hills & Dam

Chart II

Note: Locations are identical to Chart I

TYPE OF BAIT TO USE

a–Worms/Crawlers
b–Salmon Eggs
c–Marshmallows/Cheese
d–Sucker Meat
e–Jiggs tipped with Sucker Meat
f–Trolling Gear
g–Spinning Gear
h–Flies
i–Jigs Tipped With Euro-larvae, Wax Worms or mouses

Type of Bait to Use

Locations	a	b	c	d	e	f	g	h	i
1							●	●	
2				●	●				
3	●	●	●						●
4	●	●	●	●	●		●	●	●
5	●	●	●	●	●		●	●	●
6	●	●	●			●			●
7				●	●	●			
8	●	●	●				●		
9	●	●	●			●	●	●	●

Locations 3, 4, 5, 6, and 9 are excellent year round areas to creel your limit of rainbows. Area 1 is the best area of the lake to nab brown trout on flies, whereas, locations 4, 5, and 7 are best fished for the lake trout. Overall, Twin Lakes is one of the best *year round* fishing lakes in Colorado, but don't expect to catch trophy rainbow or brown trout. The fish as a general rule average about ten inches in length (Division of Wildlife creel census data). The Mackinaw, on the other hand, have achieved weights up to and above twenty pounds. The best Mackinaw (lake trout) areas are 2, 3, and 7.

11

Other Fine Colorado Lakes To Fish

The following lakes do not include maps, charts, or diagrams, but are listed as quality fishing waters which offer a quality fishing experience.

Gross Reservoir

This 413-acre reservoir is located just off of Highway 72 near the town of Pinecliffe. It offers the Front Range angler the opportunity to get away for the afternoon (thirty minutes away from the Denver Metro area) and to fish for some real lunkers. The catch will be composed of brook, rainbow, and Mackinaw, plus a large population of kokanee salmon. Snagging for the kokanee salmon is hard to beat here because the population is hardly dented by fishermen. This is because the lake allows no boats and is open only from dawn to dusk. Additionally, Mackinaw (lake trout) roam this waterway in droves, big ones too! A 20-pounder was caught through the ice last year. Use the method with jigs and sucker meat or the Leeper Keeper Adjusta Hook bait rig method and expect to catch a large fish.

Turquoise Lake

This 1500-acre reservoir contains many cutthroat, rainbow, brown, and Mackinaw trout plus a substantial population of kokanee salmon. Fish this lake as you would nearby Twin Lakes. Take I-70 to Highway 24 (Leadville turnoff) and proceed through this city until you see the Turquoise Lake turnoff.

Williams Fork Reservoir

Williams Fork is very well known for its lunker browns, Mackinaw, and northern pike. This 1500-acre lake can be found by traveling on Highway 40 to Parshall (between Granby and Kremmling) and then following the signs from Parshall to the lake. It may be one of the best kokanee trolling areas in the state. The fish are not lunkers, but offer the kokanee angler a trip to remember.

Trappers Lake

This 200-acre lake will easily qualify as one of the most beautiful pristine settings in the West. This fishery is closely managed by the Colorado Division of Wildlife and is open to fishing by flies and lures only. You will catch only pure strain cutthroats. Travel on I-70 to Rifle, then proceed on 789 through Meeker. Watch for signs to Buford and Trappers lakes.

Taylor Reservoir

This reservoir sits high atop the Gunnison Valley near the Cottonwood Pass area. This 2000-acre lake easily qualifies as one of the best fisheries for Mackinaw trout. Each year many are taken in the 20-pound class. Additionally rainbows, large browns, and kokanee salmon are on tap here. Expect to see elk and deer in the large meadows near the treelines as you fish. Take Highway 24 to Buena Vista then turn onto 306 over Cottonwood Pass to the lake signs. In the early spring or late fall you must travel to Gunnison to the town of Almont to get to this lake as Cottonwood Pass is closed for the season.

Red Dirt Reservoir

Try this reservoir for brook and rainbow trout in the ten- to sixteen-inch class with some larger fish caught on nighttime streamer flies. This is a great place to take your family. The pressure is light on this reservoir because it is hard to find, any automobile can easily traverse the road. Take Highway 40 out of Kremmling to the Gore Pass cutoff (Highway 134), then proceed toward Toponas to the turnoff for Red Dirt Road. Travel on this road until you see the lake sign (about ten miles). Curiously enough the lake sign is not on the Gore Pass Highway nor at the turnoff at Red Dirt Road. This probably is the reason that it maintains itself as a quality fishery. No fees are required and you can camp and fish right next to the lake.

Round, Percy, Lost and Long lakes

You will never forget the beauty of these high mountain natural lakes. On Round and Percy you will find patches of waterlillies atop the surface and visualize scenery only seen on postcards. Fishing is primarily for fat brookies and a limited number of rainbows stocked in the past. Lost Lake contains some large brookies and rainbows to three pounds. Find these lakes by traveling west of Kremmling on Highway 40 to the base of Muddy Pass, then turn right on Highway 14 to the small town of Coalmont. Watch for the sign for Grizzly Pass, follow this dirt road to the top of the pass. Watch for signs to Long Lake and follow this road to the roads end. Round, Percy and Lost Lake are approximately two and one-half miles from the end of the road at Long Lake.

Crescent, Mackinaw, and Island lakes

These lakes are for the hardy who want the ultimate in a wilderness experience. You'll find large Mackinaw in Crescent and Mackinaw and brookies and cutthroat in all three. The Island lakes can be reached by a trailhead at the inlet of Mackinaw and about a five mile walk down into the valley. Expect to see rams and some large bull elk as you traverse down the slopes. Take Highway 40 to Kremmling to Highway 131 (Gore Pass Highway) to Burns and follow signs. Lakes are located between Sweetwater Lake and Derby Creek. A four-wheel drive to Crescent is possible, but you can walk faster.

Seepage Lake

This may be one of the best kept secrets for lunker trout yet. How about this for statistics—the average length for rainbows caught here is twenty-four inches and the average length for native cutthroats is twenty-five inches. These statistics are from information compiled from creel census division records and printed in the book titled, *Fish and Hunt Colorado's Best*. There is an upper and lower lake. Fish Upper Seepage Lake with large night flies at night, be sure the night is moonless, and be prepared to catch fish between five and fourteen pounds. These fish are not plentiful but this lake sustains itself as a quality fishery year after year. You'll catch more smaller fish than the large—use the method that I recommend in *Colorado Trout Fishing: Methods and Techniques* for fly fishing with a spinning rod and bubble—and the recommended streamer flies to use and you'll catch one. Travel to South Fork, west of Del Norte on Highway 160 and speak to Clint Quiller at the Rainbow Grocery (873-5545). Clint will provide you with specific direction to this lake.

Jefferson Lake

In the past this lake has been difficult to reach because of the deplorable condition of the road. In September 1988, a new road has been completed which should allow access to vehicles without four-wheel drive. This lake is a deep lake of 145 acres in which rainbow, brook, and huge Mackinaw may be taken. Dan Loudenberg "The Mac Man" has seen Mackinaw break the water well in excess of twenty-five pounds and has had some on his line that he couldn't even hold. This lake has the potential to house a Mackinaw so large that it could break the state record. To find this lake travel on Highway 285 to Jefferson and follow the signs to the lake.

LEEPER KEEPER ADJUSTA HOOK

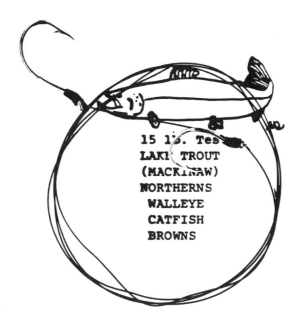

15 1b. Tes
LAKE TROUT
(MACKINAW)
NORTHERNS
WALLEYE
CATFISH
BROWNS

12

Colorado River Systems

Colorado has a vast number of river systems throughout the state. Most offer the angler solitude and little competition. Since it would be difficult, at best, to map and chart each system and the preferred spots, I will list a few systems, preferred locations, how to get there, and indicate what your likely to catch.

Arkansas River

Located below Salida on Highway 291. Fish from Salida to Cotopaxi. Rainbows, browns, and cutthroats are the fare. Brooks can be caught where the tributaries flow into the Arkansas.

Blue River

From Silverthorn to the confluence of the Colorado River. Lots of pressure. Best last two miles of river before confluence. Must ask permission from land owner and you may fish here.

Colorado River

Colorado River is excellent for large rainbows and browns on hellgramites, flies, and bait in Gore Canyon just above Kremmling. Walk railroad tracks through the first tunnel and begin fishing.

Fryingpan River

Best below Reudi Reservoir where eight- to ten-pound rainbows, cutthroat, and browns reside. Catch and release only.

Gunnison River

Excellent fishing opportunities exist from the Crystal Dam outlet through the Black Canyon of the Gunnison. From Crystal Spillway to the canyon mouth any baits can be used—from the canyon mouth through the canyon, it is flies and lures only.

Lake Fork River

Out of Gunnison on Highway 50, turn at the sign for Lake Fork. This is Highway 149, proceed until you cross the Lake Fork River. Fish from this conjunction to Blue Mesa Reservoir. Browns, rainbows, brooks, and cutthroats.

Rio Grande River

Southeast of Creed on Highway 149, fish where the South Fork River empties into the Rio Grande. Large brown and rainbows are available here.

San Miguel River

West of Telluride where Sakada Creek crosses Highway 145 and meets the San Miguel River is really good for large brook, brown, rainbow, and cutthroat.

South Platte River

Take Highway 105 to Sedalia, then proceed on Highway 87 to the South Platte River. Large browns, brooks, cutthroats, and rainbow are present year round. This may be one of the top ten trout streams in the nation. Fish it soon though, because if Two Forks Dam becomes a reality, the river will be flooded permanently.

Mary and Mert at Dillon waiting for the night fishing.
Mary jigging for Mackinaw at Granby Dam.

13

Introduction to Ice Fishing
or "How I Got Hooked"

The M&M Connection

Dark storm clouds swept across the twilight skies giving way to a calm clear winter day. A new day, a new beginning is about to unfold. I first met Mary at a coffee shop. I remember clearly that during our first conversation I stated to her that I wasn't a fishing fanatic and liked things such as the theater and such. Then I asked her to join me in a family dinner composed of a seven-pound rainbow trout.

It was at this dinner when I asked Mary if she would consider an ice fishing trip with me. She asked me if it was cold, my response went something like this, "Cold, well, sometimes at Granby Dam it gets below freezing, but I've never really gotten cold." I knew she had never been to the Granby area since she had come from Boise, Idaho only a few months earlier and surely she did not know that nearby Frazer was almost always the coldest spot in the nation.

Two weeks later we packed our gear and began our trek. Upon arrival, I immediately began bulking up (long undies, jeans, a thinsulate flight suit, plus insulated coveralls on top, a coat with hood, two burglar/ski masks, three pairs of gloves, and my arctic moon boots—purchased from a worker on the Alaskan pipe line. Mary gave me a puzzled look—I responded with the comment, "You never know what the weather is going to do up here," and "you can always take a layer off." We were in a tree-lined shelter, parked near Dike #3 and I knew when we got onto the ice that the cold would intensify. Mary thought that she was prepared. She grew in front of my eyes, one layer after another. She said, "Okay, I'm ready."

I said, "Why don't you put on this extra flight suit of mine and use my size 11 spare insulated boots. We'll put wool socks on your feet until your foot fits the boot!" At this point, I wondered if she thought my statement about not being a fishing fanatic was true or not.

Once we hit the ice, she was glad I insisted upon the layers. It was thirty degrees below zero without a wind chill factor. While drilling holes and rigging rods, I did my best to instruct Mary about how to fish for Mackinaw. And for about 180 seconds, I even showed her, dropping her line through the ice hole, letting it settle, and jigging—all the while, knowing that I'd better get to my own ice holes to get the monster Mackinaw that I knew was there.

I didn't even get my jig to the bottom when I heard Mary say, "I've got one!" Her first Mack ever stretched out to twenty-three inches. The day went something like this. I would get to my ice hole, put down my jig, and immediately hear the same words, "I've got one!" In fact, by the end of the day she was almost hoarse from repeating these words so many times. It was love at first bite. Not only was she beautiful, lovely, intelligent, and sophisticated, she was a great fisherlady!

As the weeks passed, my ice fishing companions began to expect to see Mary on the ice, jigging away. On one particularly slow day, Robert walked over to Mary and said how nice a day it was, but the fishing was sure rotten. At this instant, Mary said those now very familiar words, "I've got one!" Robert just shook his head and walked away dejectedly.

On May 21, 1988, the "M&M Connection" was complete. I wish to announce to all, the marriage of **Mary** Childs Meyr to **M**erton DeWayne Leeper.

Ice Fishing For Macks
And Other Trout

Usually about the second week of January I can stand it no longer, I've even begun to see fish in my dreams. All of the lakes have finally iced up by now and are safe to walk on (but check carefully). I'm personally not comfortable with a six-inch cover because of soft spots, but feel very safe when it exceeds eight inches.

It's interesting to note that the water temperature at the bottom of lakes where an ice cover exists is 39.2 degrees. Therefore, we have an immediate indication of which species of trout are most active at this time of the year. For instance, the *ideal* water temperature for Mackinaw is 50 degrees, whereas for brown trout it is 60 degrees. All other trout fall between these parameters.

With this in mind, it is reasonable to expect the creel census to consist of Mackinaw (lake trout), brooks, cutthroats, and rainbow. Browns are extremely sluggish at this time of the year and bite only when the bait happens to fall within a very short distance of their holding area.

Wintertime fishing offers the angler a tremendous opportunity to catch a trophy of immense proportions or the opportunity to catch many smaller trout with little competition.

Ice fishing rigs look like they are made for "hobbits." They are only one to three feet long and set up for an open bail reel to avoid the freezing problems of the closed-faced reels in winter. To this set up must be added a small wire tip (when fishing for smaller trout), but not when fishing for Macks. The reason for the small wire tip is because at this time of year the preponderance of trout species are sluggish and they don't react the same way as they do in the open water months. This wee tip is needed to see the strikes, the smallest bob could mean the largest fish you've ever seen.

An ice auger is an absolute necessity to get through the ice. I would suggest that you gear toward one between eight- and ten-inches in circumference. To give you an idea of how large an eight-inch auger hole is—my thirty-two-pound, eight-ounce Mackinaw came through easily, even though it completely filled the hole, this fish had a twenty-eight-inch girth. Anyway, once the hole is made, you'll notice a large amount of slush floating in your hole. The only way to adequately get rid of the slush is to use an ice skimmer.

Another helpful device to have on the ice is a depth finder. I have a nonpapered visual graph—LCD type. You can actually see your bait sink to the bottom, locate structure, and see all fish clearly. The key to successful visualization on inland lakes is to use a 20-degree transducer which allows a large portion of the bottom to be seen. For instance, at a 60-foot depth, over 25 feet of bottom is monitored for fish activity. If you used an 8-degree transducer, it would narrow the visual field to less than 6 feet in diameter.

Baits consist of jigs tipped with grubs, Euro-larvae, or active red worms; lures such as the jigging rapalas;

small spoons such as the Swedish Pimple; and the "Leeper Keeper Adjusta Hook" bait method. This method consists of a two-foot leader and two professionally hand-snelled hooks (the end hook is solid, whereas the second hook slides freely on the line to accommodate various sizes of baits). For Macks, an eight- to ten-inch sucker or filet of carp is just about right.

From the chapter on water phenomena, *Colorado Trout Fishing: Methods and Techniques*, it is now clear which species are the most active in the winter months and at what depths they can be found. With winter water temperatures as low as 39.2 degrees at the bottom of the lake, the Mackinaw is the most active trout species. Their ideal water temperature is 48 to 50 degrees, but their active range is from 42 to 50 degrees. This is why so many Macks are caught through the ice in the winter.

The methods for fishing for these Macks are somewhat unique. Once you have drilled your hole, allow your jig which is tipped with sucker or carp meat to cascade down into the depths until you feel slack—this is an indication that the bait has hit bottom. Once on the bottom, take up the slack, balance your rod, and begin a slow meticulous rocking jerking motion never letting the jig off the bottom more than twelve inches. A strike using this method is unique. You only feel a pressure, thus, many people who fish for Macks never really realize they are having strikes.

The Leeper Keeper Adjusta Hook (sliding hook method) is to be used while jigging one hole and watching your other rod. The rig is illustrated and described in *Colorado Trout Fishing: Methods and Techniques*. This method is especially effective on lake trout when using whole suckers. It is actually the preferred method, but as you'll find out, suckers are in demand and not easy to find (especially in the winter months). This is why sucker filets are used, they simply go farther.

Anyway, you'll note that the second hook freely slides up and down the line to accommodate any size sucker. A ten-inch sucker is a great bait anytime of the year. Hook the sucker up in the following manner.

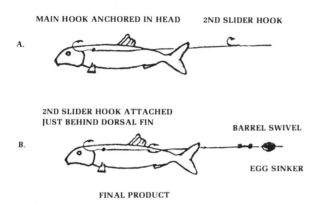

MAIN HOOK ANCHORED IN HEAD   2ND SLIDER HOOK

A.

2ND SLIDER HOOK ATTACHED
JUST BEHIND DORSAL FIN

BARREL SWIVEL

B.

EGG SINKER

FINAL PRODUCT

Note that in winter, the sinker goes into the suckers gullet and is allowed to sink to the depths on its own through an ice hole.

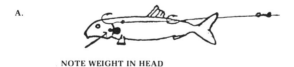

A.

NOTE WEIGHT IN HEAD

Allow this set up to cascade down through the depths to the bottom. Once the rig has settled, open your bail—your line *must* be completely free of tension and then

Dan Loudenberg with 1988 trophies. The Leeper Keeper Adjusta Hook and sucker were used to catch these fish.

wait. When your line begins to uncoil from your spool, just look, don't touch! The Mack has your bait in his mouth and is beginning a short run in which he is turning the bait to swallow it. Once the first run ceases, *get excited* and near your rod, because when the next run begins it is for keeps—Mack has swallowed your bait. Before you hit, allow twenty to thirty yards of line to pay out, then hit the fish hard (fish caught using this method in winter with big baits usually always exceed ten pounds). Play the fish carefully, for the time of judgment will happen at the surface of the ice. Use a heavy glove to grab hold of the Macks mouth—gaffs or tail snares are currently illegal—don't put your uncovered hand into a Macks mouth unless you want some very deep cuts from teeth that range from one-quarter inch and longer.

The two methods described in this text should allow anyone to catch large Macks consistently all winter long. Dan Loundenberg, "The Mack Man" and I usually do not keep any Mackinaw of less than fifteen pounds and then only to occasionally eat or mount.

14

Cleaning, Cooking, And Mounting Trout

Cleaning

Cleaning a fresh caught trout seems pretty much self-explanatory except that I have seen it done several ways. The norm though is to (1) cut from the vent to the gills and under the tongue area then remove the innards or (2) to cut from the vent to just one-half inch fron the area where the body and gills join and cut the gills where they join the body under the mouth.

The best method is (2) because all you need to do to remove all innards is to simply make the cut, place your thumb and forefinger at the base of the gills where they join at the inside base of the head and pull. Everything comes out plus the first two bottom fins are removed. Then clean out the blood line at the base of the spine. Your thumb nail will do a better job than a knife and will not damage the tissue.

VENT

CUT FROM VENT TO BASE OF GILLS

1. GRASP WITH THUMB & FOREFINGER—
BASE OF GILLS INSIDE OF HEAD NEAR SPINE.

D.

NOTE THAT FINS ARE ALSO REMOVED

Do not submerge your cleaned trout under the ice, they will deteriorate. Place them on a small trash bag on top of the ice.

Many trout fishermen or their families do not like the taste of trout. Some say it tastes too fishy. The strong taste comes from the skin. To avoid this, skin the trout. If fresh, they skin as well or better than catfish. Simply insert a small knife just under the skin from vent to tail, continue around the base of the tail fin, proceed past the dorsal to the front fins, and pull the skin off.

Cooking Trout

I usually like to have a fresh fish dinner upon my return home from an outing. Here is a recipe that will make your spouse and friends think that you are indeed a gourmet chef.

Trout a la Leeper

1 cup soy sauce
1/2 cup honey
1/2 cup white or red wine
1/2 cup white vinegar
brown sugar
parsley
liquid smoke

When you have mixed this marinade together (except for the parsley), pour it into a baking pan large enough to accommodate the fish. Make sure the pan has a lip to hold the marinade. Put in the fish—turn them each half hour for two to three hours. When you turn them be sure to spoon marinade into the cavity. Just before you put the fish, marinade, and all into the oven at 250 degrees, sprinkle the inside of the fish with parsley. While baking, spoon marinade over the trout. Bake until done.

This recipe works great for barbecuing and as a smoker recipe.

Mounting Your Catch

The goal of all fishermen is to eventually catch a fish large enough to mount. If you utilize all the methods and techniques of *Colorado Trout Fishing: Methods and Techniques*, and fish the locations described in *Colorado Trout Fishing: Part II*, you will eventually catch a trout large enough to mount. The following will describe some tips that will help you to preserve your trophy until you can get it to the taxidermist.

A. Decide which side of the trout shows off best, then place it with this side up.
B. Wrap in a wet towel, taking care not to damage any fins.
C. Place in a plastic trash bag upon the bed of ice. Be sure the towel stays moist and cool.
D. Upon arrival home, you may take your trophy directly to your taxidermist or freeze it as you have transported it.

I prefer to take a fresh trophy directly to the taxidermist. But, freezing it may be the best alternative if you do not know of a taxidermist. This will give you time to call several of these shops, compare prices, and make your decision.

It is important for you to see a taxidermist's work and compare prices before you leave your trophy in their hands. Prices range from $6 to $12 an inch. The quality of the mount doesn't necessarily denote the cost. Additionally, many taxidermists finish only one side of the mount—leaving the wall side without an eye, gills, or some semblance of color. I hardly recommend that you choose a taxidermist who finishes off both sides in terms of eyes, gills, and tail. Your mount then will reflect a depth not present in one side mounts.

Information

Colorado Trout Fishing: Methods and Techniques
Find Out _Why_ 10% Of The Fishermen Catch 90% Of The Fish

Chapters include: The Prey, Equipment, Water Phenomena, Bait Fishing, Flyfishing with a Spinning Rod, Flyfishing with a Fly Rod, Fishing with Artificial Lures, plus addendums on Kokanee Salmon, Wintertime Fishing, and Other Species of Fish.

Detailed diagrams throughout this text include: tying a professionally snelled hook; rod and reel repair; how to tie blood knots, blood droppers, trilene knots, improved clench knots, the Leeper Keeper Adjusta Hook; blowing up worms; easy ways to catch crickets and grasshoppers; volumes of unique fishing techniques for lakes and streams and how to fish for lunker lake trout (Mackinaw).

Colorado Trout Fishing: Part II
Find Out _Where_ 10% Of The Fishermen Catch 90% Of The Fish
Send Orders to:

ML Publications
P.O. Box 593
Littleton, CO 80160

Reorders of both texts may be obtained at the above address.

Mert collecting his own suckers for bait.

DATE	PLACE	FISH	WEIGHT

DATE	PLACE	FISH	WEIGHT